FANFARE

This book is dedicated to two outstanding poets
who died in 2014, 2015

Anne Cluysenaar (1936-2014)

Elizabeth Burns (1957-2015)

Fanfare

an anthology of contemporary women's poetry

edited by Wendy French
and Dilys Wood

for Second Light Network

Second Light Publications

First published 2015 by
Second Light Publications

3 Springfield Close
East Preston
West Sussex
BN16 2SZ

e-mail: info@secondlightlive.co.uk

website: www.secondlightlive.co.uk

Typeset in Georgia 10pt

ISBN 978-0-9927088-1-8

Printed and bound by CPI Group (UK) Ltd, Croydon, CR0 4YY

Contents

1   PREFACE

3   *Section 1:*   THE PLANET

3   Jemma Borg – Relic
5   Deryn Rees-Jones – Meteor
5   Jacqueline Gabbitas – Stigmaria
6   Sheila Hillier – London Light
6   Mimi Khalvati – Knifefish
7   Alison Brackenbury – Down Unwin's Track
7   Patricia Helen Wooldridge – Song in E Minor
8   Eleanor Livingstone – Snow Hare
8   Pascale Petit – Black Jaguar at Twilight
9   Myra Schneider – Seeing the Kingfisher
10   Kay Syrad – Burnt Island Lake
11   Wendy Klein – I Greet the Blue Water Buffalo of Cambodia
12   Sue MacIntyre – Remembering Elephants
13   Glynda Winterson – This Is My Wooden Elephant From Africa
13   Caroline Maldonado – Two redstarts
14   Elisabeth Rowe – Blue
14   Anne Cluysenaar – January 1
15   Anna Avebury – Freeze–framed
15   Judith Wolton – Gannet
16   Barbara Cumbers – The foolishness of squirrels
16   Jean Watkins – Shinglebacks
17   Janet Fisher – Voyagers
17   Anne Caldwell – Slug Language
18   Anne Boileau – Music of Small Things Close to the Ground
19   Joy Howard – Fernsehen
19   Myra Schneider – Lost
20   Jean Harrison – Elegy
21   Beverly Hughes – When the bees became junkies
22   Elizabeth Burns – Sea-campion
23   Janet Lees – The eye of the storm
23   Sue Rose – Damage
24   Helen Hill – Windmills at Abergele
24   Helen Moore – apples are not the only gadgets
25   Tracey Martin – Resolution on Climate Change
25   Alison Brackenbury – The mapping of the Arctic ice
26   Gill McEvoy – In the Dry Season
27   Sheila Hillier – Visit from the Sourcier
28   Kerry Darbishire – Rainstorm
29   Dorothy Ann Coventon – The River Trivellet
30   Caroline Natzler – January
30   Gill Nicholson – Portuguese Visitors In New York
31   Fiona Owen – My Father
32   Mimi Khalvati – Snow is
32   Anne Stewart – Snow snow more cold lonely snow
33   Margaret Eddershaw – Sandstorm
34   U A Fanthorpe – The Beasts
35   Caroline Carver – eelgrass
36   Kerry Darbishire – Bringing in the Shrimps

37	Pauline Keith – In the dark stable
38	Hilary Menos – Wheelbarrow Farm
39	Jennifer A McGowan – Shambles
39	Gill McEvoy – The Plucking Shed
40	Victoria Kennefick – Archaeology
41	Isabel Bermudez – Racer
42	Eleanor Livingstone – The Soul
42	Joan Sheridan Smith – The Good Shepherd in the Auvergne
43	Angela Leighton – Hollyhocks
43	Sue MacIntyre – Sunflower Harvest
44	Rennie Parker – Butterwick Low
45	Melinda Lovell – West
45	Rebecca Hubbard – Physic Garden XVIII
46	Kaye Lee – Threading the Earth
46	Jill Townsend – Cotoneaster Berries
47	Lynne Wycherley – Solstice

49   *Section 2:*   *THE HUMAN CONDITION*
conflict, oppression, families under stress

49	Rosie Jackson – The Lovers' Exchange
51	Jane Routh – The Eleventh Hour
52	Linda Rose Parkes – My Inner Ear
53	Janet Fisher – On Reading War Poetry While Listening To Jazz
53	Marilyn Ricci – Granddaughter Asleep
54	Jill Sharp – Untouchable
54	Alyss Dye – Cockle Shell
55	Martha Street – My Shirt
56	Jane McLaughlin – Assimilation
57	Moya Pacey – At the Beaumont Hamel Memorial France
58	Gillian Allnutt – Old
59	Jane Duran – Leggings, 1936
60	Audrey Ardern-Jones – White Roses
61	Angela Kirby – Foxholes
62	Fiona Owen – Man O' War
63	Rose Cook – One Thousand Birds
64	Denise Bennett – Mirror
65	Patricia Crittenden Bloom – Domestic Front
66	Mary MacRae – Life Story
67	Pam Zinnemann-Hope – Translation of a Letter from Grossvater Erich to My Mother
68	Lynne Wycherley – Inhabiting a Distance
68	Rebecca Hubbard – Physic Garden XV
69	M R Peacocke – In Slow Motion
70	Nancy Mattson – Learning The Letter Щ
71	Dilys Wood – A Miracle at Iskitim
72	Nancy Mattson – Pencil Stubs
73	Louise Green – Eli's Book
74	Lotte Kramer – Birthday Poem for My Mother
74	Helen Overell – From behind her

75   Pam Job – On 'the piercing silence of women'
75   Joan Michelson – Bosnian Girl
76   Patricia Leighton – Reporting an Empty Sacrifice
77   Gill Learner – Chill Factor
78   Jenny Morris – Twilight
79   Mimi Khalvati – The Pear Tree
80   Harriet Proudfoot – This Is How It Is
81   Ann Scorgie – Impotence
82   Susan Jane Sims – Birds in his Head
83   Jo Roach – Bird Daughter
83   Seni Seneviratne – L'inconnue De La Seine
84   Jo Peters – The Boy Who Loved Birds
85   Jenny Hamlett – In the Garden
86   Linda Rose Parkes – whenever the van pulls up
87   Vivienne Tregenza – Pray
88   Janet Sutherland – Cicatrice
90   Daphne Schiller – The Devil finds work for idle hands
90   Wendy Klein – Kid Gloves
91   Pascale Petit – A Tray of Frozen Songbirds
91   Kim Moore – The Knowing
92   Charlotte Gann – Buckle
92   Ann Alexander – Watching my mother turn into a wasp
93   Pascale Petit – Blackbird
93   Jackie Hinden – To My Husband
94   Margaret Beston – Silence
94   Joanna Boulter – My Father's Life in a Glass Coffin
95   Carolyn Jess-Cooke – My Father's Mother
96   Jean Watkins – Honeysuckle Sides
97   Rosie Miles – My Daughter
98   Maggie Sawkins – Sub Title: A Visual Exploration of Fetish
99   Rosie Jackson – Recovery Stroke
100   Hylda Sims – Strangers
102   Michaela Ridgway – Ablutions

103   *Section 3: LOVE VARIATIONS*

103   Sharon Morris – Indwelling
105   Mandy Pannett – Garnet for Birth
105   Anne Ryland – Never so much as larva
106   Charlotte Gann – Silent Daughter
107   Ann Phillips – Rose Petals
108   Victoria Gatehouse – Cord
108   Jane Kirwan – Che Angelo
109   Melinda Lovell – Past the Rose Hips
110   Janet Fisher – Arlo's Song
110   Anna Adams – Scarp Song
111   Alison Hill – Dandelion Time
111   Marilyn Ricci – Cotton Thread
112   Melinda Lovell – Face to Face
113   Bernie Kenny – April 10th, 1929

113	Shirley Wright – A Day at the Seaside
114	Anne Cluysenaar – February 27
114	Lara Frankena – Zeno's Playground
115	Laurna Robertson – Kiss
116	Ann Segrave – Mudlark
117	Kay Syrad – Letter from my Brother
117	Rosy Wilson – When you dream stone, I dream water...
118	Lorna Dexter – The Photograph
118	Helen Jagger – Leaving home
119	Cynthia Fuller – Crossbar
119	Val Doyle – Remembering Daffodils
120	S J Litherland – The Discovery
121	Jane Kirwan – Without Resolution
121	Carolyn O'Connell – Ripened
122	Belinda Singleton – Second Anniversary
123	Lynne Wycherley – Glacier-Walk
124	Anne Stewart – Nightscape
124	Linda Rose Parkes – Husband Sewing
125	Joan Downar – An Afternoon
126	Jo Peters – Daisy
126	Lynne Hjelmgaard – You, Lizard-like
127	Alison Brackenbury – And
128	Angela Kirby – Syszygy
129	Fiona Ritchie Walker – Northern Territory
130	Hilda Sheehan – Nudibranch
130	Justina Hart – A Wire to Grief
131	Rebecca Goss – Virginity
132	Kim Moore – All My Thoughts
132	Maggie Norton – A Late Love Poem
133	Carole Coates – Crazy Days 9
134	Sue MacIntyre – Deep Forest
135	Lucy Hamilton – Mal Culottée
136	Margaret Beston – By Heart
136	Diana Moen Pritchard – Barefoot in the Snow
137	Rosie Jackson – Room of the Three Windows
138	Wendy French – Knight Move
138	Dorothy Yamamoto – Honshū bees
139	Janet Sutherland – Five things I saw before my mother died
140	Kathy Miles – Gardening With Deer
141	Joanna Boulter – Dyeing the Corpse's Hair
142	Daphne Gloag – The radio clock
143	Joan Michelson – Vision
143	Jean Hall – Night
144	Wendy French – Red Sarong
144	Anna Adams – Everlasting Expanding Rings 1
145	Gill Horitz – Birdsong in Budapest
145	Elizabeth Burns – A Life
146	Penelope Shuttle – Task

147	Kim Moore – And The Soul
149	Mimi Khalvati – What it Was
150	Katherine Gallagher – Jet Lag
151	Moniza Alvi – Hanging
152	Margaret Wilmot – Hermetic
153	Victoria Pugh – Grey Matter
154	Deryn Rees-Jones – Trilobite
155	Kate Foley – A Perfect Rain
156	Yvonne Baker – The gift
156	Katherine Gallagher – Birthday Owl
157	Deryn Rees-Jones – A Chinese Lacquer Egg
157	Gillian Allnutt – Ignominy
158	Katherine Gallagher – After Kandinsky, 8 Tension in Red – (1926)
158	M R Peacocke – Notes on a Bonfire
160	Anna Adams – The Self Portrait
161	Jemma Borg – The mathematician
162	Pat Marum – Funambulist
163	Kathleen M Quinlan – Royal Engineer's Wife, 1944
163	Jean Watkins – Boatbuilder
164	Hilary Jupp – Path
164	Sue Aldred – Felt
165	Jenna Plewes – Catch and Release
166	Wendy Klein – Bird
167	Judith Cair – Raku
167	Elizabeth Burns – White
168	Jill Eulalie Dawson – Owl
169	Caroline Maldonado – The Lost Library of Jesi
169	Gill Nicholson – All These Heavy Books
170	Julie Sampson – Somewhere
171	Angela Kirby – Scaling the Herrings
172	Aviva Dautch – Moorish Home
173	Kathy Miles – Word Clouds
174	Susanne Ehrhardt – Song
174	Sarah Westcott – Lambskin
175	Clare Crossman – For the Woman who goes Swimming every Day
176	Jemma Borg – Song
176	Rose Cook – Falling on my Feet
177	Anne Ryland – After Green
177	M R Peacocke – Simile
178	Di Slaney – Reward for Winter
179	Maggie Sawkins – Antarctica to Tamazepam
180	Sue MacIntyre – Waking Elegy
181	Genista Lewes – Pastoral
182	Pat Watson – Epiphany
183	Cynthia Fuller – By Way of Silence
184	Dorothy Yamamoto – The mushroom shed
185	Gill McEvoy – The Bee-Swarm
186	Hilary Davies – In The Neuadd Valley, Brecon Beacons
187	Mary MacRae – Visitation
187	Caroline Natzler – Life's Work

188   R V Bailey – Cautious
188   U A Fanthorpe – Aberaeron
189   Penelope Shuttle – Quiet Street

PREFACE

Fanfare takes forward the representation of women writers in the anthology *Her Wings of Glass** to include many new poets from the growing numbers of women publishing poetry. It is in four sections: *The Planet, The Human Condition, Love Variations, Enquiring Minds.*

The poetry scene in the UK has changed dramatically for women. Today, our three poet laureates are women, many awards and prizes go to women poets and women are represented among decision-makers and judges. Through fifty years of exponential growth, the stimulus, the release, the growing sense of entitlement for women entering a previously closed-shop, has been palpable. The movement has broken barriers of age, education, 'class', ethnicity, and these factors have enhanced a sense of progress.

Given this progress, why a women-only anthology? One reason is to keep up the sense of momentum and enthusiasm, not least among women poets, and to celebrate the achievement of a very wide range of poets. Though prominent poets may not need another showcase, there are many lesser-known women poets whose work deserves, not only to be read for itself, but also in the context of the widening scope of poetry by women.

Already, the breakthrough of the 1980s and 1990s has changed in direction. Though with important exceptions, the early period of expansion showed a 'niche' tendency. Many women poets united on two fronts: the freedom of 'free verse' and the potency of feminist ideas. Poems about female biology, sexual orientation, relationships, our sense of oppression and awareness of new freedoms poured out. 'Confessional poets' included men but a strong bloc of women writers claimed centre stage. Later, many women did not abandon 'personal poetry' but widened their range. Broadly political concerns – for example, the environment and recent military conflicts – changed the balance. *Fanfare* aims to illustrate this broader focus.

In 1990, a recognisable 'woman's approach' was evident. Some major women poets did not 'fit the bill'; others did, and many followed their lead. But is there any difference between poetry habitually written by the two sexes today? The question may be open, but one significant factor apparent when editing was that the best of women's poetry still conveys excitement, ambition, confidence and willingness to experiment... No cynicism and *fin de siècle* attitudes here!

The poetry world never side-lined women entirely. Through the ages, women of genius got their lucky break; but suppression methods were effective across the globe and, today, in some cultures, still prevail – reason enough for a specific focus on women's writing. Here, though, we are more concerned with the future. As women settle into a novel role in this major art-form, what are the trends in the revolution that 'took off' less than 50 years ago?

WENDY FRENCH, DILYS WOOD

Her Wings of Glass, editors Myra Schneider, Penelope Shuttle, Dilys Wood, Second Light Publications, 2014

Section 1:   THE PLANET

Relic

Bell Laboratories, New Jersey, 1965

One whole year on our hands and knees,
clearing pigeons from the curious ear
of the antenna, listening for silence

under the city's noise and the pulsar's roar
and still this sound as weather makes at a door,
a low worry everywhere, burrowing

into the hours from the immovable darkness,
uncurling its strong horsehead,
until we catch it, finally, as a telescope does

in its wide dish, until we hear it
for what it is: this sound of creation
whose infinitesimal enormity

is now a thin travelling irritation;
this sound of time clocking on
and now corroded into this radio-hiss.

Jemma Borg

from *The Illuminated World*, Eyewear Publishing, 2014

Meteor

And this is how everything vanishes,
how everything that vanishes begins,
the hinged moment looking forwards and back.
Like that night when we sat with the back door open,
the summer distilled to the scent of jasmine,
the scrape of cutlery, the chink of glass.
A robin stirred in the dusty hedgerow.
Clothes held our bodies as a mouth might a kiss.
Then the meteor brought us to our feet:
a stripped atom, trapping electrons
to excite the darkness with its violet light.
I remember how it disturbed the heavens,
burned against the air to leave no trace.

Deryn Rees-Jones

Stigmaria

It's there always, a kind of reassurance,
this beautiful grey root. It will be lifted,
dusted, placed back with love, a history
of love, a simple needing of its presence,
and looked at every day. Only the heart
remains of it; became this precious fossil.
Think of the beauty in the once fine crossing
of its rootlets, lost now and calcified as scars.
Think of the crudest breaks where the pressure
of earth was absolute. Think of its resurrection,
and how you hold it resting in your palm
(itself warm and generous in the measure
of tissue, skin and bone), and give protection
to its systolic past, protect its acre of calm.

Jacqueline Gabbitas

London Light

If the night sky in February were clear
I'd see Orion and the bulls eye Aldebaran,
brilliant Gemini and crossing the span
of Pisces, Venus going to the dark hemisphere
beyond the sun. Lower than anyone could ever hear,
there are songs from when the world began,
black holes are humming a bass pavane,
56 octaves below middle C, wide, austere.
But London light is syrupy, too strong
to see or hear through, it exhausts the night
creates insomniacs, throws out a glare
across flowers, making short shadows along
balconies, grass yellow at midnight;
siphons the world away within its stare.

Sheila Hillier

Knifefish

Lit, lit, lit, lit are the estates at dawn:
honeycomb stairwells, corridors, landing lights,

flare paths for passengers flying home.
Three jets like electric fish streak the sky with rose.

Black ghost, ghost knife fish, how many days
since you went abroad, lurking in your murky pools,

locating dawn by sonar, by electric fields alone?
To image your world in darkness – driftwood

casting distortion shadows – no matter how weak
your receptor organ, faint its discharge, barely a volt,

through tail-bend, waveform, you fire, you feel,
sensing lightning, earthquake, your own kind

turning their dimmer switch up and down,
for this is how you talk. Old Aba Aba, grandpa,

with your one room lit at a time, feeling for walls,
navigating as surely as in the brightest, highest dawn!

Mimi Khalvati

Down Unwin's Track

And the rain stopped. And the sky spun
past the hills' flush of winter corn.
The mare strode out as though still young.

You walked. I almost said, last year
I saw a hare run with her young
just past the broken wall, just here.

Two flew in circles. First, one rose
upon its great back legs. It boxed
at air. The second flinched, then rose.

England has blackbirds, mice. To find
these strong black shapes makes the heart race,
as barley, under icy wind.

Boxing is courtship, failed. One broke,
tore past us to the rough safe hedge.
She crossed the sun. Her colours woke,

ears black, back russet, earth new-laid.
Her legs stretched straight. The late showers made
bright water fly from every blade.

Alison Brackenbury

Song in E Minor

The owl we bury here, by the shooting
bluebells, and the mistle tempers
his three note song, high overhead –

a minor key of softened warble – how
beginnings will begin and feed
this hunger of living,

her death cradled in my hands – still warm –
her broken neck – too low – too late – scooping
from the middle of the lane in my ungloved
hands – such tawniness – stroking.

The mistle thrush clear on the tip
of bare poplar, speckled breast catching the sun,
his trig point song, calling.

Patricia Helen Wooldridge

Snow Hare

They placed him on his side
a silhouette against the pillow, skin
stretched over long thin bones

his limbs in constant spasm, as if
he might still jerk himself awake
like a dog chasing dream hares

leaping fences; and I followed
through that cold February night
covering wordless mile after mile

a whole country mapped
between us, fields and mountains,
lochs and burns, half frozen rivers

and an outline up ahead, white
on white, passing out of sight.

Eleanor Livingstone

Black Jaguar at Twilight

All day I waited for him to appear.
Now – everything is arrival. The minutes
cascade into a dust-slicked pool.

The coming night glows with eyeshine,
a velour tapestry of mygale eyes,
this emerald tattoo of fireflies

Aramis has brought on his coat.
His paws are talus slopes of wreathed plateaus,
his gaze their severe summits.

The trick is to stare through my reflection,
to squeeze through the grains of glass,
even slip time's membrane.

The self that approaches him must shuck
its human skin, wear a veil of fiery rain.

Pascale Petit

Seeing the Kingfisher

It may be that I stumbled
on the burning blue moment
because I'd stopped trying to find it.

One leafless December morning
as the sun sifted the uncertain air
I glimpsed blue in flight and gleaming

above the Brook's polluted waters,
a sapphire blue but unlike stone
it seemed weightless, movement flinging

spectrums of colour. I thought I'd misread
magpie feathers or maybe dreamed
the bird that I'd turned into myth

but it alighted on a twig by the stream
and I saw its breast's orange swell, its blue
paler in the shade, its size smaller

than I'd expected. For one minute – two
it perched motionless, then dived.
Heart racing, I questioned why

I'd longed to see the actual bird
when a photograph could show it larger,
more clearly. But I knew the truth:

I needed to catch sight of it alive
in the untrappable now. I walked on
through pools of sun. At the last bridge

I saw two pairs of luminous wings flying
upstream above the unruly rush
of waters muddied and swollen by rain

towards the trees by the viaduct.
Could this vision help me entertain
with calm the thought of a coming time

when my conscious body will fold away
and I'll be feather-thin images that fly
into minds and perhaps settle there?

Myra Schneider

Burnt Island Lake

When he heard the pure, long calling of the loon,
   a strong swooping majestic call, early,
when the loon had dominion over the black lake,
   only the loon and its echo beyond Tree Island,
he tried to place it with another sound:
   Régine Crespin singing Berlioz, perhaps;
and when the loon called once more,
   three muscled, rolling syllables, he thought:

one of Charcot's hysterics in a high French room.
   Yesterday, at Alder Lake, he'd been trapped
in a gold swamp by beavers' dams
   and he'd cursed the beaver as it swam towards its lodge
for he'd hoped to see a moose in the forest,
   to match its big round paw prints
with the shadow-prints of the water boatmen
   curiously enlarged as the sun met the water's surface –

instead he paddled back to the rock-and-sand
   promontory where he slept in a tent with his wife.
'Try just listening,' his wife had said,
   touching his mouth with her fingers,
 and they'd listened to the whirr of a humming bird,
   two red squirrels chasing each other
in the pine trees, water against rock, flies,
   and the wind in its private rushing.

He was bored with listening.
   He read his book, just his sort of book:
a European journey, both acerbic and romantic,
   and he sat with his back straight
against a tree in Algonquin reading about Poland,
   New York and Vancouver, the 60s, 70s,
the years when he too began to place things,
   when he began to rejoice in equivalence.

But his wife had thrown off her clothes,
   her limbs had turned golden under small waves
and the sunlight was making her glitter.
   He wanted to follow her, wanted to be
that glittering figure in the water.
   He edged forward, like the little hornet
with its sticky pads—but already his wife
   was dry, throwing trail mix to a chipmunk,

gathering wood for a fire. He retrieved his book
   and flicked through the pages,
reading about exile, thinking about symmetry
   (and the two fine lake bream he'd caught
for their supper). Then he could hear the loon calling
   again and he closed his eyes: a series of long,
echoing loops, the echo of the loon bringing
   the lake inward, calling the lake to heel.

Kay Syrad

I Greet the Blue Water Buffalo of Cambodia

O you are blue, not the casual blue of everyday sky,
the shade a child crayons in above a house
with a chimney and windows for eyes,
not even lapis lazuli, too decorative,
but blue enough to drown in.

O you are so blue, not the faded blue of denim jeans,
run up in a rush by a girl too young to work,
nor the periwinkle blue of tucked-away
blossoms in lands you'll never see
where your yoked presence is not
known or even dreamed of.

O your blueness is so much deeper than powder blue,
though far short of midnight, closer to sapphire,
cornflower, steel. Yes, steel blue is the sheen
of your flanks, smoothed over muscles that
undulate in time to your master's demands
as you plough his rice paddies to feed
his family, the world.

Wendy Klein

Remembering Elephants

A summer trying to remember elephants, how they visited
their dead, their laying on of trunks, how they fondled the tusks
of the dead, staying on and on. In my mind still seeing them,

oblivious in caravan, between the pillars of Kings Cross Station
and the rushed concrete of other dead places, as I trail
up and down England with my rucksack, my L.L. Bean bag,

like a student with a railcard and the mirage of family.
Those elephant ways of moving and thinking, how will I
hold on to them: the baby between the tree trunk legs,

the moving forest slowing down for him, the moving island
coming back for him, wickerwork of sun on
leathery backs, sun lighting up the baby's forehead

as they trample past villagers' houses, stripping trees
and tearing up bushes, lumbering steadily
and trumpeting their sorrow?

Sue MacIntyre

This Is My Wooden Elephant From Africa

I don't think you'll be implicated
if you look.

Its tiny tusks, no longer than a crescent
cut from your fingernail,
are hand-carved ivory.

I never guessed the violent attack,
a hacked face
left half-scuffed into the ground,
one eye staring through a fizz
of flies. I never heard
its last trumpeting.

I was just a child
taught to say thank you.

I took into my hands
the souvenir my parents' friends
had brought for me from their safari holiday.

Uncertain how to play with my new ornament,
I wrapped it in a clean white handkerchief,

laid it to rest
among my wide-eyed dolls.

Glynda Winterson

Two redstarts

From under cupped roof-tiles
they've slipped onto my doormat –

sleek Valentino heads and rufous tails
like the flare of a buttonhole rose,

yet side by side they resemble a couple
on a Sunday morning lying in.

Caroline Maldonado

Blue

She brings him the egg still warm in the nest of her hands,
a perfect freckled blue like the eye of heaven.

Holding it gently between gnarled finger and thumb
he pierces it with a needle, north and south,
makes a soft egg-shape with his lips and blows:

the filmy dribbles of silver, the threads of gold
quicken a fledgling hurt she cannot name.

One day in her perfect blue emptiness she will remember
the crushed shell in her hands like pieces of sky
flecked with blood, the assiduous thrush still singing.

Elisabeth Rowe

January 1

It made me look in the shed, his cooing: too early.
And he had her by the neck, sure enough, a wing
across her back. They formed a tremulous mass,
the two of them, snowy white, in the dim shed corner.

But because, of my life, the present is only a part,
I've watched for the eggs, the two she lays one by one,
and fingered them out from under her beating wings.
No skinny squab must starve as winter sets in.

For these, alive in my hand, holding their heat,
there never was hope. Though tempted to put them back,
I know that, soon, there are bound to be flakes of snow.
Better throw them across the yard to the bramble bank.

They'll be food for sparrows and rats. Even so, as I slipped
my hand underneath and felt that hot patch of skin
each side of her breastbone, I heard myself mutter 'Sorry'.
And know how relieved I'll be when the snow does fall.

Anne Cluysenaar

Freeze-framed

Soundless, the serpentine
rippling of its wings as it hovers
over the ditch, head tipped
left, then right, fixing its prey;
tail-feathers scooping the air
into its wings' embrace.

Almost motherly, its tending,
riding the breeze; the ratchet
tightening for the kill.

Deadly, its gorgon gaze.

Anna Avebury

Gannet

How did you get here –
spread out in mid-dive, flat
on an alien beach?
This isn't your territory,
this isn't your seascape –
our shore's too shallow
for your arrowed plunge.

Yet here you lie,
breast on sand,
seemingly perfect;
your yolk-stained head
turned sideways, displaying
that spear-blue beak,
gimlet eyes soft shut.

You who could battle a storm –
how were you carried here
to our soft sand
and morning sun?

Judith Wolton

The foolishness of squirrels

It's not yet ten o'clock and already
the heat is pressing its dry weight
down on head and lungs. Already

others are preparing to camp
in the shade of the cottonwoods,
avoiding the whiteness of afternoon.

There's a thumping behind me –
a squirrel is whirling its tail to drum
on the ground, and chattering.

In the shadow, an inch in front,
is a rattlesnake, coiled and still,
diamond head solid and deadly.

The squirrel is deliberate
with its feckless little noises. Perhaps
the god of squirrels is a rattlesnake.

The squirrel is in awe of it, dancing
before it with the pointlessness of ritual.
I wait in shamefaced hope that the snake

will strike, but it goes on sleeping
and I walk away, downwards
into the white noon of the canyon.

Barbara Cumbers

Shinglebacks

Down under, the ugliest lizards in the world
drag their bodies and thick broad tails along
the scrubland. Like a length of scaly conifer branch
with stumpy legs, they go slow. Slow.

But wait. They mate for life, the male trundling
behind his love. One narrow boat towing another.
She struggles like any mother's daughter to push out
her young, two or three, head first.

And when in a roaring cloud of dust a truck wheel
runs over a lazy lizard, which happens often,
its mate will stay for hours by the corpse,
nudging it gently, waiting for life to resume.

Jean Watkins

Voyagers

'All nature seems at work. slugs leave their lair'
S T Coleridge, 'Work without Hope'

Where are you off to, night seekers?
The dying year doesn't leave much
to munch on: old moon daisies, bolted
lettuce, ivy fingering over stones.

Coming home on damp evenings
we skirt your slime, avoid squelch
and slip of flesh, fresh black
or long slithery orange.

By day you're humble, glorious throats
struck dumb. You hide in dry grasses
flexing your jaws till moonrise
and cool dews summon you.

Janet Fisher

Slug Language

Kitchen, 3am

Pure tongue,
their bodies write out
the glow of a pearly button
burst from a pale silk shift,
the sheen of a vulva.

They have criss-crossed my lino
all night, wound together like a nest of snakes
to smear the soles of my feet
with their silver calligraphy.

I print the whole house with desire.

Anne Caldwell

Sun after rain, Whitsun bells shout –
we're walking home after church –
in their Sunday best the snails are out:
barley sugar, bullseyes, butterscotch.
Sparkling jewels with stripes.

The grown-ups go on up the hill,
as I watch my snail with her delicate horns.
Now I'm the size of my big toe nail,
I'm gliding beside her, I've taken her form,
my shell grows warm as it dries.

We are at home wherever we are,
and all is wet and warm and well.
We travel slow but can travel far
in the safety of our stripy shells,
through stitchwort, harebells, rye.

I hear the creak of ferns unfurling,
the whirr of a bee-fly trapped in a web,
the squelch of waking worms uncurling.
I smell damp earth, mosses, sedge.
A raindrop has captured the sky.

Mother's lace-ups – she takes my hand,
and we walk up the hill to Grandmother's house.
Can you catch the snails? Here's a bucket of brine.
They hiss, withdraw, spit out green foam.
I watch them float and die.

Anne Boileau

Fernsehen

All the colours and the conflicts
of the world are in my sight
but a corner of my eye escapes the glare

catches a glim of gold-dust flight
climbing the penlight slide of sun
piercing the curtain shield

a small invader prone to do great harm
whose hatchlings threaten
my cashmere   my best velvet

and I should clap it in my hands
finish its glittering dance
along the dusty sword of light

but am entranced   a captive
released from wars of attrition
for three entire minutes

Joy Howard

Lost

after Chagall: 'Adam et Eve chassés du Paradis'

There is no music now in paradise.
The garden's ripped by cries of consternation,
a blinding white circle of face belongs

to a figure whose body is flower-blur
and stems twinned with leaves, a figure
inseparable from this place, its din.

There is no music now in paradise.
Tranquillity is a shrivelled fruit, trees
wrenched from roots are hurtled to the sky,

birds plummet to ocean, stampeding hooves
smash grasses. The tempter's vanished,
panic-bitten humans are in flight.

There is no music now in paradise.
The word *sin* hisses in ears, guilt
lays its eggs, hearts work like clappers,

selves are in tatters. Though daisies
will rise again, moments gleam with sound
there is no music now in paradise.

Myra Schneider

Elegy

Go home
shut your eyes   remember the silence
of a day without wind

grey tree trunks shining in heavy air
buttressed then smooth
up to the lowest branches of a black canopy

a path where pink flowers lay browning,
crush them against your face as you did that day
know what petals lose when they fall

count the cries of a fruit-dove,
listen to leaf-shade as it mottles bark
mould as it subsides

part a tangle of five-fingered leaves
spot clinging underneath
knees bent   white eyed   tree-frog

pull your foot back   a sea of ants
each one grips an egg like a rice-grain
the way a dog carries a stick

a screech   black wings with yellow stripes
bills like capsized canoes
sail across

heavy white trumpets   lilies spot-lit by sunlight
I brought some home   their scent
permeated every room

too much   now
the great trees have been felled

Jean Harrison

When the bees became junkies

Last Tuesday,
not all the bees came back.
Their daily sugar search drags on across town,
now the countryside's stock has gone.
The last flowers stripped months ago,
licked out, dropped, like used paper cups.
In out-of-control swarms
bees hunt in the car park,
or hang around by the fair,
to find their next fix.
Their once furry stripes wire-stiff,
with dribbles of fake sweetener.
Wings dull as used tissues
unfold like yesterday's papers.
On streets sticky with unseen chemicals
like spilt invisible ink,
they suck up cherry lubricant
citrus toilet cleaner, meths,
fruits of the forest shampoo,
anti-freeze, lip gloss, coke.
Then carry their cargo back
to the hive to unload.
Too drugged to notice
they've been short-changed,
their honey's blue and green,
not gold.

Beverly Hughes

Sea-campion

Only when you get it home
and set it in a glass of water
with the mouse-ear and the sorrel
do you notice something queer
about the flowers:
petals ragged and mis-shapen, asymmetrical
and oddly clustered,
the silk of flower-skin crumpled.

You remember seeing paintings
of wildflowers next to nuclear sites,
how they were mutated and deformed,
and think of where this campion grew:
on a low ledge of cliff at the edge of the bay
round the headland from the power-station
which empties its waters into the sea
eight times each day.

You remember how your daughter sat
and made in the sand little graves
'for mice,' she said, and decorated them
with shells and stones and flowerheads,
then made a smaller one,
'for mice who die as soon as they're born'
and a tinier one,
'for mice who die before they're even born'.

And you think how the tide will have risen now
and the water with its silent freight of poison
will have washed away the sand graves
and be reaching up now to the grass,
soaking into the sandy earth,
touching the tendrils of plants,
seeping its way up through the roots
and into the delicate spoiled flowers.

Elizabeth Burns

The eye of the storm

She stepped into my room
wearing nothing but a self-coloured tattoo,
a firework bloom flung
across her body in skin filigree

It's a lightning flower, I said,
staring at roots that snaked into the dark
half moon of her waist. *I've seen pictures
on the internet – and this is a dream*

It's a tree, she breathed, quiet
as leaves falling on the knife edge
of November. *The last but one –
and you're awake*

Janet Lees

Damage

The sky is full of cadences,
bird call, wind swell,
clouds in shifting alliances

herding shadows over the fells
as they cross the ungeometric blue.
Beneath, we trek summer trails

past fields of stone-eyed ewes,
lambs in the greasy lee of their wool,
impervious to the news

that, up there, hangs a pall
of volcanic ash, high
as ozone and invisible

as damaged cells to our naked eye.
Stalled routes, the stopped engine
of the skies, are the only signs

it's there; that, and the skin
of extinct fire: a greying
over every thing.

Sue Rose

Windmills at Abergele

They rise,
a strange white army
ranked along the coast
where Edward's castles stand.

Our new invaders,
spinning wind into light,
hold past and future
in their outstretched hands.

Helen Hill

apples are not the only gadgets

jaguar is not a big cat of the *Panthera* genus, the threatened
feline of the Americas, but a high-performance engine,
its exhaust notes a snarl, an iconic car, *a vision for our future*

apple is not a pomaceous fruit typical of orchards
but a multinational company that designs and markets electronics,
computers, software. (Child labour worsens in its Chinese factories)

winnebago is not the name of a First American tribe
(known also as Ho-Chunk), but a motor home, a lifestyle with compact
coach, rotating 20" TV, vinyl ceiling, and wood effects in mocha cherry

blackberry is not a fruit comprised of drupelets, common
in hedgerows, but a smartphone with apps to change the way
consumers live, work & play. Apparently they *do more – faster*

touareg is not a Berber people, the nomadic pastoralists of the North
African Sahara, but a stylish off-roader that *takes you anywhere you want to go*
(advertising: state-of-the-art hyperbole)

earth is not our wider, life-sustaining body
but a cache of raw matter to be stripped, mined, fracked,
made machines to appropriate the native

Helen Moore

Resolution on Climate Change

after Copenhagen 2009

In the last two minutes of tomorrow
the last sliver of the last glacier
will slip into an ocean lapping
at the walls of Timbuctoo.

In the last two minutes of tomorrow
the last leaf will fall
from the last tree, unnoticed,
to the smoking forest floor.

The last hunter will kill
the last tiger lying in
the burning grass. The last flies
will buzz around the wound.

In the last two minutes of tomorrow
the last lion will lie down
with the last lamb, both
no longer able to eat.

And the last lovers will light
their last candle beside
the bed in their dark house,
hiding from the dangerous sun.

And in a mountain hideout
the last two politicians will argue
over the last two words
of the final draft.

Tracey Martin

The mapping of the Arctic ice

Less had gone than I thought. The edge is ragged,
like a cake a blunt knife trimmed,
and such a cake, whose chocolate glistens,
fruit pulp melts in the Jersey's cream.

Careless, you stretch. The knife slides on,
slices air.

        The cake has gone.

Alison Brackenbury

In the Dry Season

The earth is parched and shrinking,
even the grass has given up its hold.

I think about water – we are all thinking about water –
there is a hosepipe ban in force, and stringent
warnings to be frugal in our use of it.

I measure out mean cupfuls from the tap,
imagine (my body ninety percent this element)
each cup as hand, foot, forearm.

On the windowsill above the sink
a jade plant, fat green money tree,
is flourishing,

every leaf a reservoir of hoarded wealth,

while *rain* now seems to me a word so beautiful
I roll it on my tongue like a wildly expensive taste,
chant it like a mantra:

rain, rain, rain, rain,

as if in calling I could make it come.

Gill McEvoy

Visit from the Sourcier

Not twenty-five. Black hair and long brown hands,
the *sourcier* from the neighbouring village –
and his arm in a sling! *Madame, it makes no difference.*

Cold master-wind *mistrau* rips at the grass
perturbing it. He bends, straightens, stands still
a full minute, *Madame, the mistrau doesn't matter*

then heads off, crosses the long field and where
his Y-shaped stick turns up, he plants a stone.
I follow, placing flags that wave like poppies.

At the boundary wall he turns back, stares at me,
his eyes are deep, *Madame, dig where you like,*
this field, though dry on top, is full of water.

Do I believe, *sourcier, sorcier*? Is he better than chance?
But I have felt it too, sometimes it seems the house
floats over a lake which draws our bodies' water down.

Hill-streams feed networks underground; *Madame*
they say our springs are all connected from
before time, to the great basin below Mt Ventoux.

The thought compels me: all our foundations
lie on water, those earthy tributaries flowing out to sea
through salt caves, facing into the rising tide.

Sheila Hillier

Rainstorm

Sky blurs, lowers like a press.
Rain-drops group like lyrics
stamp the parched hillside,
turn sheep into boulders
   churn peat into becks
      dust to mud and soon in the yard

hens stoop to half their size
with feathers glued.
A gang of jackdaws swoop barn eaves
– cocky boys in shiny gear.
   Grass and buttercups sink in plaits across the field
      mice and leverets flush out

and won't stop at hedges scattered white –
blossom trashed like stirks have belted through.
Walnut buds jump to turf,
barn rafters leak, buckets fill
   gutters sing
      and ring like xylophones.

In walls of ivy, blackbirds
roof hatchlings fat with worms,
lupins, monkshood, roses list like masts
in a herbaceous sea mist,
   afternoon
     is drenched in perfume.

Behind crinkled curtains of rain
we wait for slates to hammer out
a slower beat, for slugs and frogs
   to celebrate – dare to slip and dance
     like leaves along the path.

Kerry Darbishire

The River Trivellet

at St. Nectan's Well

As if running, and before herself,
the river spit-screams over the ledge,
shouts a spate into the black slate funnel,
and roars to a rock basin that
pours breaking water
onto the quietly breathing altar
of the well.

She's still now
her light-mirror saucer reflects
the Late Devonian dome. Sprouting trees
root where the birds dropped them,
their supplicant branches disguised
in wish – and – grief – rainbow ribbons,
left there to guide
whispered prayers.

Crystals implore on slippery ledges.
An amethyst rosary hails Mary
on dried Sycamore leaves.
A blue elf waits in such devotion
by a small moss covered –
once fragrant –
unstopped bottle, that leans
on an icon, of a girl so thin
in a waterproof frame, that somehow
keeps her memory dry.

The pool is slow to let go,
trees, ribbons, and sun-rayed dome
stay devoted to its light-mirror
levitating on keen pebbles
and humble coins,
agitated by the undertow
and the headless Saint
that walks her water to the sea.

Dorothy Ann Coventon

January

Going into the sun
over mud flats skimmed with water

people are walking on ice or glass
their reflections perfect

and you know it's a new year

walking into the sun
beach and sky cast in light

sheer

gone when you turn

and wave rippled mud
takes your footsteps, softly.

Caroline Natzler

*Portuguese Visitors
In New York*

    for Phil

Christmas Eve it snows.
Flakes the size of half-crowns jive.
I've not seen crystals like it,
says the Prof, *what's more,
I doubt I will again.* The Portuguese
look up, eyelashes wet
with silver hexagons.
Snow is a mystery to them.

If, in a future time, rare flurries fall
far north on melting ice,
or at the centre of the southern pole,
how will we value them?
In sixpences, in dollars or
in worthless brilliant diamonds?

Gill Nicholson

My Father

     with his voice raised to heaven.
My father on his knees in an icy field
fists shaken at the sky, snow threatening,
like a god brought down who knows his fate is sealed –
while we, his children, hands in pockets, kick frozen sods
nowhere.
    It was futile we knew the pickaxe he'd wield
to bury a pipe would bounce (it did); of all the jobs
to do that day after weeks of hard frost
that one was most against the odds –
the earth rang as he struck the ground till he tossed
the tool hard against the barrow which clanged
like a lonesome bell. My father's temper lost
he fell to his knees: *Holy Christ*! His roar rang
and he railed as the snow sailed down around us,
a kind of benediction, softening the strong
will of the man. We, gathered in a hush,
an uncertain circle around him, felt something like awe –
hero or fool we couldn't be sure.
      Then in a sudden rush
of recovery he rose in the dusk from his little war,
remembering us, his icefume turning fast to thaw.

Fiona Owen

Snow is

Snow is a rubbing of sorts, a wax heelball on ground,
an impress of ribs – exoskeletons in high and low relief.

Each snowflake is witness to the cloud-womb that formed it,
how wet, how warm, the union of crystals, how powdery.

Trapped in firn, air will evidence ash from Krakatoa,
deposits from lead smelters, pollen and greenhouse gases.

Snow is adjectival. On foliage particularly, discriminates
between the feathery and lobed, the linear and pointilliste.

In itself is silent, but on contact, creaks. Acquires an air
of sanctity in repose but in action earns oaths and profanities.

Snow is a friend to children, those who have scarves, mittens,
snowboards and wooden sledges. To others, it is the devil's own,

akin to the djinn who frequent sinkholes, wherever mud rejoices.
To the children housed in sheep sheds, chicken coops, tents,

dressed in cut-up blankets, seeing things that aren't there in forests,
snow is the devil they know. Better him than the live bombing.

Mimi Khalvati

Snow snow more cold lonely snow

Snow the pillow snow the cloud
snowed-in snow the jailer snow the shroud
snow the weapon that selects you hurts you laughs out loud
(oh, yes...! that same snow that cried incessantly before it froze)
snow the bright smiler the dead of winter's glitzy clothes
its curves its sonsie sashayer its belles
– and beaus – it doesn't care – it only knows it's here
can't wait to flaunt its frisky cheer-you-up
and show you just how innocent magnificent
a dirty boy or girl can be – it's snow!
It has its flaws and foibles just like every angel
every all-grown-up each saint each one of you and me
it doesn't like assumptions as to who or what
– or how obedient to conformity – it ought to be
Don't you remember being snow?
Snow the beautiful the fearsome intruder snow
the ASBO snow you're stuck with snow that makes demands
the funside snow that wants to play and never tires snow
you may as well admire – if not its naive adolescent stand
at least its all-star-cast-we're-only-here-till-Friday
fabulous flip-you-sideways show.

Anne Stewart

Sandstorm

A thumbed pie-crust of sandstone
ripples the skyline,
smooth hips and dimpled flanks
of dune-sculpts sunbathe
then in a quiet wind they start to smoke

Round a scoop of emerald water
oasis palm-trees turn belly-dancers
arms flung above startled skirts
deep hollows whip-lashed
into boiling cauldrons
a world changing colours
4WD tracks instantly erased
as we creep forward
grains spiral against the windscreen
nil visibility
wheels spinning
engine furious
a sliding figure of eight etched
as we attack the ascent.

Through the dark veil
a faceless Touareg
tall on his white camel
that sways on knobbly legs
overtakes our Toyota
floats up the slope
fades as if rubbed out.

Margaret Eddershaw

The Beasts

After the flood, they left the Ark.
(Two by two. Hurrah Hurrah Hurrah)
Noah had saved them. Life was good.
(All together now. Hurrah Hurrah).

Noah had a vision of his sons
(One and two and three. Hurrah Hurrah)
A vision of fur and tusks and skins,
Of rifles, poison, harpoons, gins,
A whiff of battery hens (Hurrah Hurrah),

Draize-tested rabbits, cattle trucks,
(Thousands and thousands. Money for us. Hurrah)
Myxomatosis and abattoirs,
The pheasant shoot, the *corrida*
(Money and death. Hurrah Hurrah Hurrah).

Noah remembered the forty days
(The Arkful of precious lives. Hurrah Hurrah)
Tiger, panda, bittern, cod,
He knew how dear they were to God
(Who made them all. Hurrah Hurrah Hurrah).

He knelt down so the worms could hear
(No one counts worms. Hurrah Hurrah Hurrah)
He said, *You creatures great and small,*
My sons will soon destroy you all.
Scram! But they didn't scram nearly far
Enough.
      (Hurrah
           Hurrah)

U A Fanthorpe

eelgrass

not a thought in my head
only eelgrass
slippery as a new-caught fish
arching on the riverbank
and my heart says
>   *do something or I'll break*
>   *and you won't like that*

so I train a beam on the fisherman
sharp as a laser   strong as the moon's tidal pull
till he thinks
maybe this one's too small to bother with
or   I'm on one of those rivers
where you have to throw them back
which is what he does

leaving me wondering how they feel
after a succession of hooks
have torn those soft cheeks

how they keep falling for the same old trick
as they pass on the *must-grab-that* gene
to their babies

and how so many men
inherit the desire
to catch everything that comes their way

dream of pre-Raphaelite naiads
descending a staircase
in long flowing gowns
smiling
fishhooks hanging out of their mouths

Caroline Carver

Bringing in the Shrimps

When the ground crunched like shells
and breath hung still as a frozen cloth
Les knew it was time. A man of land and sea
    – ate only what he could carry.

   Come on lad, he'd call

pulling my man from warmth into the November night
to drive along the bare coast road where people had done
with walking for the day, where trees curved
    like net-mender's hands.

Into the sift of salt-white pebbles they marched
abreast of the tide pressed dark far beyond shifting sands
and where the sea held its breath
    set their nets on the bar.

With half an hour to scrape shoaled gullies – timing the turn
just right then back with a catch of phosphorescence
– a mass of heaven
    steering into the bite.

We laid white sheets in the moon-shine yard, set wide pans
of water on the stove. My children woke soft-eyed and
wrapped in blankets to watch the sacks of grey turn pink-gold
    in the boil – a spread of ancient tender swilled onto linen.

Kerry Darbishire

In the dark stable

the ghosts of heavy horses
sometimes shift (Black Tommy,
Bay Tommy and the mare
without a name); they shake
the harness hanging still
from hooks high on the wall
above her head. The child
works near the doorway
in low light filtered
from the slaughter-yard
where real dead animals
lie stretched. She's helping
with small jobs she's fit for:
ladles dog-grease into jars,
smoothes them flat full.

She scoops live maggots
into old tobacco tins;
heaped, they wriggle flat
before they're capped
ready for the fishermen
who come from the canal.

If one falls free, she lets it go,
sees how it loops along,
in cracks between the flagstones.
It doesn't stand much chance:
one way open air and birds,
the other back inside the yard
where it hatched on a fly-blown haunch.

It risks bucketfuls of scalding water
dashed down to sluice the flags
of blood and treacherous bits
that make clog-irons slip.
Not as cruel as a hook.

Yet she reaches for another tin:
her uncle and her grandfather
don't care, screw down fast, so
half-maggots fall, twist on the floor.
Mine don't die like that.
She gently scoops more maggots,
tips them in and waits, lid poised.

Pauline Keith

37

Wheelbarrow Farm

When hell freezes over, he swears by three things.
Lard on the lips. Two pairs of socks. His wheelbarrow,
good on the steep when even the Ford won't grip.

This morning he opened the door to a clean sweep
right up to the dairy's cracked slate step, frost
spangling the tank and, briefly, he's ten years old

but now it's taking the piss. Grunt glares at the snow
and it glares back. He kicks the water trough,
heels a hole through the ice. First floods, now this,

the daily round, in arctic sludge. Milk substitute
for the calves, a brick of pellets for the fowls.
He rolls out a silage bale in the cubicle house

and forks it to the cows, sets a can at the yard tap
drumming up chilly water for the dogs,
for the lambs in the barn, the fifty hogs on the hill.

A neighbour phones on the scrounge for a box
and a tow out of the ditch where he spent the night.
Grunt goes off to do what he does best –

apply excess force with a tool. He's back at noon
to fix a burst pipe, by which time two sheep
haven't moved for an hour, are past fixing.

Snow starts to fall as he toils up the slope,
hauls one sheep into the wheelbarrow,
picks his way down, then moils up again.

Hilary Menos

Shambles

Told not to look through the lattice-work
under the porch, my mother did.   She was five.
Her uncles –
                        You have to understand.
It was a crowded house, just post-war;
a poor area. Her mother's six half-brothers
miners, hunters who would shoot dinner
and slap it bloody on the kitchen table
in front of her, jeer she was too good
for her supper. They raise chickens
in the basement, said her mother. Don't look.

Chickens fleeing round that butchers' heaven.
Brute uncles laughing and the thwack of the axe.
For days afterwards, sleeping, half-asleep,
she saw dead chickens, running. Pulsing.

Jennifer A McGowan

The Plucking Shed

As we pluck, the air fills with a flour
of feather and dust. Everyone sneezes.
The floor is pillowed in down and quill.
Our footsteps smother in the folds of snow.

The plucking goes on, and what you are
beneath your plumage shows itself:
enormous prickly pears,
feather-pores like craters in your skin.

On the floor your other selves,
the white plumed creatures
that we knew as geese,
grow light and tall:

each time the door is opened
soundless skeins of ghosts rise up
and thread their way
into the blanket of the night.

Gill McEvoy

Archaeology

Dr. Andrey Poyarkov studied Moscow's strays for years,
watched them zip between legs of bustling travellers,
catch rides on the Koltsevaya Line.
He observed them navigate from suburbs
to the city, choose the first or last carriage,
bound on seconds before the doors shut,
risking their tails. 35,000 stray dogs commute,
pant out time, never miss their stop.

Before the fall, they lived on the outskirts,
searched for food in garbage dumps,
lived on whatever workers threw away.
Now commercial centres, restaurants
and fast-food outlets huddle downtown,
so dogs are smarter, they obey traffic lights,
find kiosks where men shave meat,
canine-tongue thin.

A middle-aged man buys himself shawarma,
chews it without rush on the bench, pops up
when one of the pack barks;
the tasty snack falls to the ground.
A lanky teenager loses the same way.
Moscow strays have their own subway statue;
commuters rub its bronze nose for luck.
On the train, Dr. Poyarkov writes in his notes:

There were no dogs before us –
our first bones found in Russia, 35,000 years old.
A dog for every year.

Victoria Kennefick

Racer

She trembles when she sleeps, shudders
toward the track, chasing the lure; all haunch, ears back,
reliving the roar of an evening crowd;

smell of beer, glint of signet ring; shadows
of men who trained her. Six races won, second twice...
But in the orchards of her later years, she keeps to the path,

never long out of sight. A year or so ago, she might
have hared after rabbit, disappeared under apple-trees,
a streak of flank among the green.

Now is it death she sees, when she stares
into a field of baby rabbits and barely stirs?
At home, lies there, dreams; crosses and uncrosses

long faun legs, or rests her head in my lap
for no other reason than affection it seems,
till she hears the jangle of collar and catch

then she's out again, under Kent apple trees
to mooch round windfall in evening sun
her lead swinging empty from my hand;

nose to the ground, riddling old scents; trailing
the trigger of the starter's gate in the haze of the finish line;
September's first chill meets August's ripe breath.

Isabel Bermudez

The Soul

after Rilke

His ears lift up
tugged by wires from above.
He waits, nose wet and shining,
sinews in his legs and back
straining towards the darkness
beyond the station lights.

Each hair of his coat is ready,
in full course, *courant*, tail stiff,
eyes – oh, his eyes,
ears tugged,
           tugged
by those wires, four paws
holding the platform down

until at last the train arrives
and hope flickers this way and that
with tiny nervous pulses
scans each face. Each face passes.
Pass friend. He waits. He waits
on guard, a soul unguarded.

At this cold juncture,
late at night,
beyond all rational hope

he waits.

Eleanor Livingstone

The Good Shepherd in the Auvergne

We met him going up the mountain,
as he was coming down. Tall, vigorous,
sure-footed, ruddy from his outdoor life,
he cradled in his arms a new-born lamb.
He greeted us, and smiling tenderly
at his small burden, simply said:
'Regardez – l'innocence'

Joan Sheridan Smith

Hollyhocks

for my mother

All summer now they've climbed through their own dying
flower by flower to the topmost lookout posts.
They've notched up weeks in brown, pouchy seedpods –
an abacus of what will be thrown to the winds.

Late summer saves them. Warm, windless days
uphold a last dignity of flowers.
What do they see? Their regard overlooks us quite.
Long sight belongs to those who scale the heights.

The best is past. Their wide papery stares,
like periscopes to what lies over,
tipping these stems that bend to the weight of them –
the lightest tissue of a life flowers at the utmost.

Angela Leighton

Sunflower Harvest

This time I came to the valley in September.
It was filled with another crop, the crop
of the total eclipse of the moon,
the machines going heavily at night

under bright lights, harvesting tobacco.
And the sunflowers? Before,
the land was splashed with their yellow,
irradiating huge spaces, opening doors,

their erect heads anxiously turned
to stare at the sun. Now they are crumpled,
brown as bats, necks bent, small heads
down, such a spillage of self, such a shrinking.

I felt they were you: when you came
to the door your face showed more than grief,
your world out of joint, as if a harvest was
nothing more than a spilled seed basket.

Sue MacIntyre

Butterwick Low

Alas, *girasole*
it is the wrong time of year for you.
Your torches are extinguished
in a line from Marjoram's Motors to Deeping St. Nicholas.
There is a place called Malice Farm,
there's another place called Tongue End
and the birds are pecking your eyes out
in the blackened stumps of January.

Meanwhile the turbines are lording it,
they cartwheel across the fen
slicing the wind to size –
and you are more forlorn than ever,
the chewed bristles of an old brush.

I am wishing you slow summers
under the pressing heat.
I am hoping to see your gargantuan heads
follow my car as it glints past
on the stagecoach route to Spalding.
But now you are the bent skewers after the barbecue,
what's left of the trashed cabinet.

Alas, *girasole*
the tractor is coming for you
and the road-salt gritter is worrying on
with hot stones rattling at its heels.

Rennie Parker

West

Wild poppies, swathing westward,
in our furthest west, you have ignored
our grand design. The thinner the wayside soil,
the more abundant your zeal

This patch of soil is ghost-tilth,
thin as shakings from a sieve,
the poorest, most common soil
with no leavings of nitrogen,

so miserly that your seeds germinate
in hundreds. Hairy stalks are crammed tight.
Only the blackcurrants rise through them,
keeping their own claim

Everything else has succumbed
to poppies, wavering but strident,
heads crooking in faded red,
toughest of immigrants

Melinda Lovell

Physic Garden XVIII

At first she wondered why the Germans had dropped
seeds as well as bombs in her garden. Swathes of
rose bay willow herb sprang up overnight on rubble
piles. Vibrant yellow ragwort, nettles, sorrel, dock and
poppies appeared on the burned-out site of their
London terrace. After flames and ruins, incredible
colour. Buried seeds re-greened the city, signalling the
way.

Rebecca Hubbard

Threading the Earth

after Mira Schendel 'Still Waves of Probability'

There is a thread
that joins the earth to the sky
a fine thread, invisible to us
yet strong, so that the earthquake
shaking rocks from mountains
cannot break it, the hurricane's wind
can only flex it – when the wind has passed
it falls back, light-ray straight
and its end-curl strokes the earth.

But there will be times,
maybe as the moon rises
after its week of darkness, or as a sunshower
crosses our window, when we hear
a small voice, a cloud's whisper
saying: *Look now!* and we look
and see a thousand threads,
and we know our world
must be cherished.

Kaye Lee

Cotoneaster Berries

Less prized than holly
at this time of year
yet intense clusters
and reddened leaves
on spokes and fans
wheel against the fence.

These are the beads
blackbirds tell, a rosary
against dark winter nights
when a woman with imagination
might burn her lips on one
or, tasting, scald her tongue.

Jill Townsend

Solstice

Half bat, half moth,
it hovers at the lychgate

not first light
but the presentiment of light

love's silkworm.

Through a rib-cage of pine trees,
the rhizomes of my fingers

the sun-child rehearses
his yellow song

a citrus face
beginning to be born.

And life is writing itself:

new tracks to stoop to and name.
Rabbit. Thrush. Cleaves of deer.

Intaglios. My own prints
walking backwards

to somewhere on the edge of light.

Lynne Wycherley

Section 2:   THE HUMAN CONDITION
conflict, oppression, families under stress

The Lovers' Exchange

He traces the scar on her knee, indigo still
from the playground's coal dust and gravel.
She wonders at the small V over his heart:
a girlfriend's angry scissors.
The marks on her wrist he passes over silently,
touches the hollow of a lost child.
Lets her caress the scorch on the back of his hand
from when he was eight, an English boy living
in Germany, and the man in the barber's shop
stubbed his cigarette in the young white flesh,
said: 'That's for Dresden'.
She puts her lips to that place
where the fires burn all these years on,
as if her mouth, her one breath,
were enough to blow out the candles of war,
return to their bodies newborn skin
on which nothing is written.

Rosie Jackson

from *What the Ground Holds,* Poetry Salzburg, 2014

The Eleventh Hour

Armistice Day 2003

There are leaves still on the trees
near the mountain hut, Mont Blanc framed
perfect against blue sky. In Yellowstone
you can see only stars. It's night
in Auckland too: those are its lights
glittering across the bay from Devonport.

The South Pole's out of action, all turbulence
and wind. Mawson Station's on:
portacabins in primaries, rock, snowdrifts.
No one outside. Pale sky almost green.
Ascencion looks abandoned: 27° – dawn I think –
a white dory pulled up the hard, a wave.

Macquarie's frozen, a Sisley of lilac
greys and green, but Antarctica's left behind
its sound effects: sea ice breaks and cracks
unstoppably, a Weddell seal yawns.
Nothing from Nuuk; and in the dark, Denali's
lost to Anchorage's light pollution.

Ah yes, Bagdhad. Out-of-date
as you'd expect. A green shop sign,
an ordinary side-street. No one's about.
The text is Spanish – if I have it right, it says
all people are collaterals.
Everyone. Everywhere.

Jane Routh

My Inner Ear

Lately the door of my vowels is opening wider
to my mother's forebears,
accents of places I hear in my sleep:
the Vistula and Oder flowing
into the Baltic through the tributaries
of my diphthongs; sands and winds
and dropping pine cones, the howling grey wolf,
the scatter of scree on the mountains.

Hammerings on anvils, fricatives and plosives
from the smithy in Bielsko-Biala,
punctuate my dreams, alongside the military
band trumpet of great-grandfather,
forced into the Russian army:
tarantara ... tarantara – brass notes turning
into the New Year *s h o f a r*.

And now the cossacks galloping in, brandishing *shashkes* –
tiny Grandma crouched at the window
in the province of Lublin, circa 1908 –
mother locking doors, rushing daughter
to the back of the wardrobe. Not all the family
set sail for Swansea thirty years before Treblinka.

Here's little Grandma again, wearing a ribboned hat
she's made ... *schmutters,* she grumbles
and her seasoned shibilants salt the borscht,
the Sabbath cholent. Somewhere in the din
at the root of my ear, the clock strikes one
in Amhurst Park – the sonorous chime
of my mother being born.

Linda Rose Parkes

On Reading War Poetry While Listening To Jazz

Across the grass the stumbling
sax spills grace notes into my lap
painting the sky red. The almond air

curls round the honeysuckle,
the poplar's long shadow
a finger pointing.

Twilight: the ghost of a mother
stroking a baby's brow as he dreams.
When he wakes she's gone.

Is it separation, or fear, or the power to kill,
that makes men lonely, each in the shell
of his skull, the fallow deer haunting his dark?

Janet Fisher

Granddaughter Asleep

Jet curls frizz into bunches held by
crimson bands.   Beneath, long lashes,
broad nose, your mother's sweet mouth.
And the dark suede of your skin might
wrinkle, even now, into giggles.

Sometimes, when you don't want to leave, or
rage at the limits of being too young,
I'm afraid those cruel histories – dark ships,
plantations, famine – might be in your eyes.

But, even then, survival impresses,
etched into each tiny bone
of your face, hands, feet.

Marilyn Ricci

Untouchable

She shines like Lakshmi through the fields –
a gentle stride, arms at her sides.
By the houses, stooping her beauty
to the earth, she raises the brimming bucket,
its stench sealing her nostrils. Slurry clings
to hair and skin, but nothing changes
on her face, only a puckering of lips
in silent thanks to Kali
for twenty years of women's work,
this dawn till dusk that's nurtured seven sons;
thanks that she's never known the blessing of –
nor visited this curse upon –
a daughter.

Jill Sharp

Cockle Shell

Morecambe Bay, February 2014

One half of a hinged box,
a little Chinese hat,
an opened fan,
its ridges, once rough,
now softened by sand
to the texture of corduroy.
It has a crimped edge, like tiny teeth,
and a soft palate where my thumb fits.
Inside, it is the colour of an old lead tomb
and smooth like the steps of Santiago Cathedral
worn down by the feet of pilgrims.

Our buildings outlive us.
This one's occupant has long since gone.
But, in pursuit of him,
a soft-bodied Chinese girl
voyaged thousands of miles
only to be battered by waves,
washed up against the shore,
shell-less.

Alyss Dye

My Shirt

Blue threads link women.
In Bangladesh she wears
a bright sari of thin poor cloth

her hands move swiftly
across bleached denim
so little time lost

so little fuel or coin
needed for her quick work
in dusty slatted light.

My shirt is nothing to her
mere stuff of work work
trance of work as quick quick

through her fingers
she draws seams, tosses garments
into piled baskets at her feet.

Blue blue – she must dream
of blue – such foreign blue –
does she wonder, turning

first sleeve, second sleeve,
folding both sleeves, what other
woman's arms will slide

into this blue – no time
to raise her eyes
to wonder how, and who?

Martha Street

Assimilation

It is important to learn the language

What is your name?

They took my name at the border
I have filled in the forms to get another.

Where do you live?

I live in a street where pomegranates flower
and birds and children sing at evening.
I live in a pile of white rubble.
I live for four days without food on a jolting truck.
I live on a mattress in my friend's room.

Tell your partner something about yourself.

I tell my partner my right eye does not trust my left
and if I have two hands I am afraid
that one will kill the other.

What do you do at the weekend?

At the weekend I lie on my mattress
and listen to that silence that follows
gunfire and the fall of shells.
In the darkness I still cross borders
in strange clothes, leave friends and lover
where they fall.
At weekends I remember
I am the one who got through
and have nothing to carry except their names.
I watch the roof of a prison
that keeps closing over me.

Please listen to this conversation.
It's about asking the way.

Jane McLaughlin

At the Beaumont Hamel Memorial France

The boy's letter hangs straight on the pale wall,
'Don't cry Mary, this way we won't starve
I promise I'll be home for Christmas.'
His penmanship is upright and precise.
Steady hands that Somme morning pulling
On bright blue puttees; fingering
His caribou insignia and pleased
That he does not stink of fish.

He wants to be gone over the top
With the other eight-hundred Newfies –
Farmers and fishermen–
Dead men who stepped out
Heads bent; chins tucked in
Against the fierce snow of battle.

Moya Pacey

'It was a magnificent display of trained and disciplined
valour, and its assault only failed of success because
dead men can advance no further', comment on the actions
of the 1st Newfoundland Regiment by the Commander of the
29th British Division at the Battle of the Somme.

Old

available earth –

your fallow, arable field

your sad field, France –

whose turning and knowing

somnolence –

culpable earth –

your orchard, knurled

of apricot, mirabelle –

whose long familiar moon

men whittle at, mourn –

fallible earth –

your truthful, untruthful women –

vieille

whose gnarled lullaby

lullay, lullay –

Gillian Allnutt

Leggings, 1936

When he moves away the child is trying
to tie them, the new leather leggings.
The child's hands are soft and small.

The man has a sword, a beard, a rifle,
he is ready for anything
but these leggings trouble him –

they will measure the dust behind him.
And the child, you see, doesn't let go.
He is fumbling at the laces, struggling

and the houses down the hillside
split in the first sunlight, split open.
The work of dressing so the man's life

can be taken away from the child,
the bad sun purposeful. The man has a purpose
and the child, being helpful, helps him

in his mission, so he is stopped
from moving away for a few moments.

Jane Duran

White Roses

for my mother

She never spoke about her early life in Lvov,
she told me about shocks to numb the pain,
how she left at midnight, a last minute tipoff
escaping under covers in pelting ice-cold rain:

she spoke about ECT, drugs to numb the pain,
she left without a goodbye kiss for her mother,
escaping under covers in pelting ice-cold rain,
fearful of Russian soldiers, her missing brother:

she left without giving roses to her mother,
rushed outside by her father, no time to pack,
fearful of Russian soldiers, her missing brother,
a young trainee doctor who never came back:

rushed as a run-away, no mementoes to pack,
her fleeing a city where thousands had died,
a young trainee doctor who never came back;
most nights she prayed, said a rosary and cried:

fled a flowerless city, where thousands died,
high cheek bones, blonde hair, Polish accent,
most nights she prayed, said a rosary and cried;
viskey, spiced sausages, Madame Rochas scent:

high cheek bones, blue eyes, thick Polish accent,
addicted to cigarettes, red lipstick and cricket,
viskey, cold chicken, Madame Rochas scent;
she spent days in bed, hidden under a blanket.

Audrey Ardern-Jones

Foxholes

Back from France by small boats
and night trains
the last one stopping
to let him down in the wet fields
where he'd pick his way
through the warm breath of cows,
tensing at every vixen's bark,
owl call, twig-snap and leaf rustle,
at something half seen
behind the bramble mound,
then over the stone stile
like a final obstacle in an old game,
up the potholed drive,
past the duck pond
and in at last to the kitchen
where some mornings
we'd find him there asleep,
spark out on the dog-haired sofa.

In the creased photograph
beside his mother's bed
he leans against her,
nineteen, thin inside his uniform,
the bloodstained bandage
tight against his hair
and for years after there were times
when the dreams came back
till we grew used to it, waking
to the shouts and screams,
to the glimpses of him
struggling naked
in his damp and foxy bed

Angela Kirby

Man O' War

For my Dad

1: First

What time of day was it – I forgot
to ask – when you heard that *whiz*
(is that the word?) bullet through air
then Taff's breath suck in sharp
intake like sudden surprise (it was)

a brief wheeze then he keeled
backward fell away from the sights
a black blood hole marking the spot
cross-fire or lucky enemy shot *bullseye*
his left one gone, ruined face, bullet in the brain
it would have been quick

As he fell
        o you – younger by far than me now,
twenty in thirty nine   lean-faced, toothy,
good with words –
        you felt your body's inner roar
rapid fire, surge of flight or fight (flight not an option)
aimed your Lee-Enfield SMLE eye for an eye (smile please)
your first *mad minute* the rifle's quick kicking back
against your shoulder, bolt-action, kill or be killed.

2: Second

You came over the top and found them
in a blasted crater just after (could have been you)
mud mayhem cacophony of chaos bits and bodies

and some of them from the ground raised hands
towards you don't want to see the whites
of the eyes bewildered swinging like white flags,
wounds crawling blood bright men staggering
nein and *bitte* and *kapitulation*

Everything in you screamed *help them*
but
wounded enemy can regroup
so the order came:
shoot them.

3: After

Oh to stretch long arms back through time's black hole
to save you from – what? Not death – you came through the war,
lived a long good life   loved and were loved (still are).

Can't airlift you out, spare or deny you your history. But
I break for the soft in you. What you had to do, see, carry.

Fiona Owen

One Thousand Birds

    for Sadako Sasaki

In October, up to sixty thousand cranes
pass overhead, skeins of grey across the sky.
Here an installation of white paper cranes,
continuous rain from metal hooks,
birds dance through air, arc to the floor,
the smallest fade into the distance.

Wide windows throw sheets of light.
Sadako is in bed, aged twelve, folding her birds,
one thousand to ward off leukaemia.
She was almost two when the bomb flung her
from the breakfast table. Her family crouched all day
in a boat, in radioactive rain near Hiroshima.

Now she folds paper, this way, that way
to make a crane, folding to create the elongated neck,
the elegant sweep of wings. Sadako folds to make
a thousand birds for protection against her illness.
When she dies in October, her friends complete
the cranes, bury them with her.

Rose Cook

Mirror

In the burning street a mother is shielding her children,
covering them with blankets she found in a tub of water.
A woman trips, screams as her baby flies from her arms into the flames.
A grandmother is gazing at the remains of a blackened pram.
The bombers find their way home under a cinder sky,
guided by the red light on the west tower of Ely cathedral;
a flock of screaming devil birds are circling the air.
In church candles are lit for the war dead.
By hearths prayers are said for the safe arrival of the airmen.
Mother are banking up fires to welcome their sons.

Mothers are banking up fires to welcome their sons.
By hearths prayers are said for the safe arrival of the airmen.
In church candles are lit for the war dead.
A flock of screaming devil birds are circling the air
guided by the red light on the west tower of Ely cathedral,
the bombers find their way home under a cinder sky.
A grandmother is gazing at the remains of a blackened pram.
A woman trips, screams as her baby flies from her arms to the flames.
Covering them with blankets she found in a tub of water,
in the burning street a mother is shielding her children.

Denise Bennett

Domestic Front

My mother died still mourning for her life
not fully lived. Sorting keepsakes from
her disenfranchised past, I came across
a tablecloth with matching apron, chain-stitched
with scarlet flowers, neither ever used.
I'd seen them once in '43 and mother
dumb with tears.

Our father, 'over there,' immured by rank
and camouflage, directed sharply pointed
views on home-front duties and the war.
A war which scissored up our skies at night,
brought the drone of doodlebugs above
unguarded roofs, sent flames devouring church
and village homes, and drilled us daily
into queues, where butchers' whims became
the *law* – fostering household pride in
making-do.

In times of Leave, we children held our breath.
His voice a force to send us scurrying,
his tread a feared arpeggio rising on the stairs,
soldier's hands at home with cane and belt.
Only when he left for good, did the house exhale,
though our mother's face took on a crumpled look
which never left.

It's not clear when father dropped his stitchery
and needled with that steelier thread – ambition.
But we were witness to his military acclaim;
his photos in the papers, handsome, proud,
a smiling, medalled stalwart in The Presence
at Buck House.

We buried mum, drove slowly back to tea
and what remained of her long life: a rented
bungalow, a garage stacked with boxes
marked OXFAM. One held fine stitchery:
Father's needlework – like Truth – another
casualty of war.

Patricia Crittenden Bloom

Life Story

Night, and you step out into blackness, over
the side of the silent vessel, dreading that you
or your boots might slip and miss the rung, one
false move your last. Between above and below
you hang breathless, locked into history –
and this is what you chose, what you want.

No moon, no stars – though light's not what you want –
only a sound like a thumb rubbing over
corrugated card as the men in your story
run down the ladder, loaded with kit. And you
feel rather than see, where the man below
you wavers, shifts his pack, now there's no-one.

'Dropped like a stone,' I hear you say, 'just one
splash and he'd gone.' A small smile. You want
to cry, can't quite believe the man below
the water wasn't you, rehearse it over
and over again to convince yourself that you
survived the war, came home to tell your story.

It comes back to me now: hearing your story
I saw what you saw, clear as glass, how someone
plummeted down, but whether it was you,
or him, or someone else, I didn't want
to know. Slid through a door that closed over
his head, from dark above to dark below.

Whoever that man was who plunged below,
if you're the secret sharer of his story
then I'm yours. And the story isn't over;
when you dropped like a stone you left me one
part short, however much I wanted – want –
to understand the plot and why I miss you.

Taller than life, younger than in death, you
come to visit me now from way below
the spirit-level of dream; won't speak. I want
to ask if you can love me – that old story –
but don't; put my arms around you one
last time and say, I love you, over and over.

I conjured you from below by telling your story
and then I saw our two stories are one:
can I want yours to end before mine's over?

Mary MacRae

66

Erfurt, Germany, 1947

Translation Of A Letter From Grossvater Erich, To My Mother

Nimmer mehr, nimmer mehr.
Im Wald in Bulgarien
Schoss ich einmal ein Reh:
Das war in früheren Zeiten.

I shot a deer
in the forest in Bulgaria
that was in another era.

Dare I dream of the days
when I had cigarettes, salmon, wine and brandy,
the walls weren't perforated by shrapnel,
the windows weren't shattered;
a time before the green carpet was stained
with the jam that kept dropping
off my bread, every night as I walked up and down,

als ich nicht hustete

when I didn't cough,
when you were here.

When you were here
I took you to the Bulgarian forests.
That's where my memories gather
they gather mushrooms;
they gather some for me and some for you.
I've sorted them carefully, the edible from the poisonous
and a pile for the don't know.

You sent me medicines after you ran away.
You are my daughter;
it's been thirteen years since I heard from you.

I sit here coughing,
staring at piles of forest mushrooms.
Shall I leave you some

im Zimmer hier?

in this room ?

When shall I see you?

Nimmer mehr.

Pam Zinnemann-Hope

67

Inhabiting a Distance

There were days the sky lived in your eyes,
a late-winter light, white metal. Some said
you were remembering the war. Italy,
the desert. But I'd see the boy in you
and distance beckoning. Saturday fields:

how you'd flee from home, a camphor front room.
My grandmother calling, maddened, relieved
and dinner's at one! It won't keep.
Freed from a pipkin to a sea of peat,
Farcet Fen, Ramsey Mereside, the Nene.

After the war, those fields would restore
their bitter certainties. Potato-picking, ditching,
singling the beet. Your demob coat no proof
against the wind. A tractor clinging
to the skyline. Writing its one black poem.

Lynne Wycherley

Physic Garden XV

He wouldn't be any trouble, not if I know men.
Something softens a man when he lives by the earth. A
soldier but he'll set weapons aside for a hoe. Working
the land is a physic. The garden calls in the sick, they
answer like chickens to the rattle of corn in a bowl.
He'll mend by me, I'm certain. Lying in bed at night
he'll hear the plants grow: ivy sprouting through the
broken plaster, holly knocking at the roof tiles, roots
pushing through the soil under the house – white
strings that feel past the stones. Those sounds reach
deep into a man. He'll stop hating and cursing and
learn to find his way round.
Why, summer in my garden is like a high tide rising –
foxgloves and cow parsley shoot skyward. That'll touch
him. And in spring we'll tap the birch tree, watch fresh
sap pour into the cup and drink. Green tonic heartens a
man after war or winter.
But for now I watch over him. Night after night he
sleeps like a vagrant under my hedge. I feel like a
blackbird tending a nest. People laugh, I know, but I've
found what's true. Making love under the lilac,
buttercups quivering. Together we'll make the trouble
pass.

Rebecca Hubbard

In Slow Motion

She's slapping across the dust
    frame by frame
and the gutters full of sand
in her camel leather shoes,
scouring the rubble
        frame by frame
            for the place
where the dead are playing cards.

But they don't look up, they say
Go home old woman it's late,
it's too late now. Can't you see
the sun's burnt out? Our lava brains
have cooled, we're light as pumice.

It's a dream you're in, go home!
Bake us a tray of sand cakes.
– A pair of bombs – look, three straight shells –
sniper flush, a sniper flush –
Don't think you can bury us,

it's a full house already.
Game's up, and you can't deal us
a different hand. Mother, go home.
We've forgotten you for good.
Frame by frame we've forgotten you for good.

M R Peacocke

Learning the Letter Щ

I'm checking the ways to say that Cyrillic letter
shaped like a Roman three with a heelspur
or cricket stumps with a ploughshare
to cut beneath the bottom line of text: Щ

One teacher suggests I pay attention
to the double thistle in the gap
scratched between two words
whose start and finish match: Welsh sheep

Another says, listen to the scrape
of the hinge in a folding pushchair
or the mother's voice when her baby's shout
drowns out the bus's brakes: Hush child, we're nearly home

Another wants me to try the sound of steam released
when you touch the pressure cooker valve
the cheery whistle of the sealed vessel
shortening the beet time for borsch: БОРЩ

I remember the steam train
screeching to a stop at the station
delivering everyone's grandmothers, flesh-cheeked
babushka-wrapped against December's   harsh chill

I remember the shooshch
of my grandmother's tongue and teeth
sucking her tea through a sugar cube
telling her stories in Finnish

Hush now, it's the one about her sister
in Soviet Russia, how she barely survived
on watery cabbage soup: ЩИ
but was finally crushed   lost   she

disappeared
the sound is a soft *shchi*
one wave in an ocean of millions
that receded but never returned

Nancy Mattson

A Miracle at Iskitim

In Siberia, a symbol –
this is what the locals believe,
a magical birth of water:

a fresh water spring, a spurt
close to the ground, a low white
eternal flame.
           We dip our cups
(plastic, from the hotel) and say,
"It tastes pure. The water is pure."

Some people here heard the last trucks
grind out of sight, after they shut
the 'lagpunkt',
               the slow-killing place,
left the scar for people like us
in a half circle, dark barrels

in our padded coats, gloves, hats, scarves …
With our white breaths, we breathe out lives
as we raise up transparent cups,

    "The future came too late."

Dilys Wood

In her *Gulag, A History* (Penguin, 2004)
Anne Applebawm refers to a new fresh-water
spring near a former camp at Iskatim.

Pencil Stubs

She hoards pencil stubs, files them away
underneath a loosened floorboard
writes facts to her sister on the backs
of cast-off manifestos printed in Cyrillics.

She writes of her husband, dragged away
as labour fodder for a spade gang
one of thousands – who's keeping count
forget it, line them up in rags

call them skin mallets, buckets of bones
for hand-digging the White Sea Canal –
Belomorkanal – a shallow ditch
a couple of hundred kilometres

through permafrost and granite
swamp and springmelt
lined with rottable wood
such a feat of hollow engineering

that the state issued a new cigarette
to honour it, *papirosa*, the same
diameter as a bullet, 7.62 mm:
pop that in your mouth and suck.

Everyone loves a daily hit
of *Belomorkanal* – twenty-five
cheap plugs of high-tar tobacco
in disposable cardboard tubes.

Every puff of smoking pleasure
celebrates tens of thousands
of canal-builders burnt out
thrown away like *papirossi* stubs.

She stares at a shredding poster:
"Canal Army Soldier! The heat of your work
will melt your prison term!" Moistening
her pencil lead through cracked lips

she writes of a daughter, given away
taken away what's the difference
to the camp commander, spermless
and his barren wife in furs.

Nancy Mattson

This book is in Hebrew, the child says
so you must read it backwards.

The photos are in black and white
and I don't need to know the language

to interpret. This is his family's book,
a book of faces, a book of names

a book of loss. I wait for him to be
distracted by something more colourful,

and I pick up the book the English way.
I read the pages, the images, from front

to back. The clothes grow more affluent,
the faces younger, the gaunt lines of

mouths melting back to smiles. More figures
fill the frames as I turn the pages, reversing

the trajectory of passing years. The dimness of
ghetto rooms is replaced by gardens, pianos,

the grandeur of Polish municipal buildings.
The urgency of the last photographs, the need

to record themselves, the knowledge that shouts
from their eyes, is being erased. I read their story

backwards, from the last days to the first, from end
to beginning, back to before the days are numbered,

before arms are tattooed, before children are hidden;
before that first sick glowing of the yellow star.

Louise Green

Birthday Poem for My Mother

Today I have reached the year of your dying.
Again I bleed with your limitless falling.

In your enduring is night of beginning
To measure the unsure dawn of each morning.

You laboured to give me light we call living;
Your torment denied the untempered journey.

There is no redemption in slender offering,
Help me to kneel in the desert of weakness:

Only a moment from Sinai's glowing,
Only a husk of an unsponsored answer.

There is no frontier to losing and healing,
My coming-of-age breaks on summits of praying

Now in this autumn that taught me my breathing,
Appled and auburn with your first blood's promise.

Lotte Kramer

From behind her

   for Dita

Towards the end – stubbled eggshell skull, skin
cleaved to bone – on the forced march beyond the barbed wire,
her knees buckle, women either side prop her up,

all are herded into a barn, the great doors closed,
thirst cracks her lips, kindles fire in her fissured throat,
fallen ghosts keen in her sleep;

day breaks with no sound – the yard a blank stare,
faded stars in the sweep of morning;

the allies, haunted now and always, greet
wraiths with dulled eyes, wisped breath,
share out rations, do what they can;

and then the lone journey back to her country,
her village, surely her father will make his way home,
every train draws her, holds her;

another emptied platform, her hands fall by her sides,
behind her, he half-sobs her name.

Helen Overell

On 'the piercing silence of women'

from 'The Arrival in Madrid of the International Brigades'
Pablo Neruda

Well, Pablo, I sit here and try to write,
like you, of wine and conviviality;
about maize, shells, weather, feathers,
anything but those two children in Gaza
whose faces I can almost see.

The three year old girl, *with beautiful eyes,*
the doctor said, her arm blown away
and a hole in the back of her head,
not yet dead; the five year old boy,
the base of his spine missing vertebrae.

There is a silence piercing the world.

Holed up here, we hear the wails,
the sobs, the ululations.
We are soaked in images
of women going to the wells of mourning
and we are silently screaming
alongside them – can't you see us?

Pam Job

Bosnian Girl

When they had finished with her and with her mother
she climbed a tree and hung herself – a girl
in a red sweater that her mother had knitted.
This is one front page image I remember
from the Srebrenica massacre.
If we could live inside the memory of 'Once
there was a village that was undisturbed',
by now she'd be a mother knitting sweaters
for her own daughter. My fingers unbuckle
the woven belt she slung around a branch.
Her slim bare legs are swinging down.
Feet on earth again, up she springs and runs.

Joan Michelson

Reporting an Empty Sacrifice

Kosovan harvests flame
beneath an autumn sky
and caterpillar tracks
glean cabbage rows.
And you, Valmiri Delije,
are sprawled on a hillside
amongst fallen leaves.

       Valmiri Delije
       Valmiri Delije
half in, half out
of your fleece blanket,
snug in your padded anorak,
your dummy
dangling round your neck,
your small face
flecked with blood,
one plump hand raised.

You lie, Valmiri Delije,
like a tossed corn doll
feeding the soil
with your blood.
       Valmiri Delije
eyes closed, face calm,
you have not reached
the age of understanding,
show no blame or fear.

       Valmiri Delije
       Valmiri Delije
I did not know you,
I was not there,
but my fingers trace
the black/white/grey
of your newsprint image
and I cannot stop the tears.

I cut. You will stay
– here in this book –
       stay, I promise,
until it is yellow with age.
And whenever I turn to this page
I will chant your name:
       Valmiri Delije
       Valmiri Delije.
It is all I can do.

Patricia Leighton

Chill Factor

He tries to dream cool – of ponds he dared to step on
till he heard the gun-shot crack, stilled waterfalls
in Cumbria, of sleeping in an igloo or an ice hotel.

Sangin dust grits between his teeth, chafes
his shoulder blades, sticks to his sweat no matter
how much care he takes undressing, shaking out.

His final tour. It's 48 degrees: he must think cool –
frost fairs on the Thames, blue light of glacier caves,
Shackleton's *Endurance* trapped and crushed.

Heat beats at his helmet like a welder's torch,
his nape's on fire, eyes sear with watching
as the search team makes its slow way back.

His last long walk. The escort's guns are poised.
Without his body armour he steps light
along the track. Tomorrow – home, to stars

in their proper places, Cathy's frown, the garden
gossipy with birds, the children's bikes to fix.
Soft-fingered sun. Rain. He lies flat, tools

to hand. The silence grows. Now he believes
cool – in Saturn's rings, the Skaters' Waltz,
a white bear on its lonely floe. He wipes his mind,

strokes away sand and earth, starts to unpick
a knotted mass of metal, batteries and wires.
The desert holds its breath.

Gill Learner

Twilight

Evening lowers itself
beyond the meadow.
A drone disturbs you,
causes bird-twitter to stall
copse-rustlings to still.

Monotonous hum
of an unseen beast.
It treads air towards you.
A dinosaur-helicopter rears
up over the hill with a roar,
quick, low, loud, close
with flashing orbs.

You cower into smudged grass
where ants run from their nest.
You cover your face, think
of crows pecking out bright
eyes of newborn lambs.

You think of strangers
in that dark shape above
seeking you out in the gloom.
Black night would be better.
Daylight would make it
unbelievable.

Jenny Morris

The Pear Tree

And when there's no poetry in it, the hour, the sky,
only cumulus and the first faint ossicles of rain

pattering on glass like a bone bundle thrown
for a shaman to divine, when no answer comes,

faith gives up, brain slackens, skin sloughs off
like a turtle shedding old scutes from its shell,

when the same dread incubus squats on the heart,
hiding a breathing hole on the top of his head

for all breath, desire, have long fled his mouth,
when friends disappear – and were they friends? –

and your head on its single stem weighed down
heavy as a baby pear tree not with pome or pear

but with time's three globes, what then,
little pear tree, bletted by frost? A rootstock

has dwarfed you the better to bear but quince,
pear, whose bridal kiss will you perfume now?

Mimi Khalvati

This Is How It Is

Don't look. I can't look
Look. See this. See me. Still me
Touch me. Hold me. Don't touch me.
Your hands would stick.

An armour will protect me,
hold me up. I've lost my guts, my digestion
my backbone   all connection   my core.

No armour, no, it's pushing me apart
those legs that disappear, not knowing where to go.
  Armour, you are no answer. You hurt me.
You're on the damaged skin –
the parts that can't be covered, can't be hidden,
can't be healed.

I will never be together again
be able to unite head and genitals.
I have no future.
I cannot live in this
I have to live in this.
I will live behind my hidden face
not looking.

Harriet Proudfoot

Impotence

I feel like the peacock butterfly
that came in through the window
but mistook the glass for freedom.

Things I could do last year
now seem denied.
Spasms in the skin
make the body seem an uncomfortable coat,
legs like baggy trousers.

As a child I remember wooden figures
you could make go down a board
jerking along in stiff movements,
prodded and pushed down the slope.

I grieve for the person I once was.
She has become a fiction,
a travesty, no longer real.

On a good day I imagine
I can do all kinds
of ordinary things, as before,
till I try to stand up –

then I am forced to remember.
I struggle across the room
like the wooden soldier.

Through the window I watch people
walking by so easily.
Like Faustus I'd almost sell my soul
to walk out of the room.

Ann Scorgie

Birds in his Head

"My son has birds in his head. I know them now."
from 'Daedalus' by Alistair Reid

My son Tom's
got birds in his head.
In the morning a seagull wakes him,
though we live inland.
And they both demand
herrings for breakfast.

Mid-morning and if I'm watching
I'll see his pink tongue
dart in and out of his mouth
in time with a cuckoo clock
that only he can hear. Cuckoo, cuckoo,
cuckoo until he reaches ten;
my signal to have the kettle on
and the biscuits in, so he can get
at the custard creams.

At lunchtime the fingers
of my son's right hand drum
the kitchen table and the fingers
of his left tightly grip
the handle of the spoon he dips
in his pea green soup.
The noise drowns out
the woodpecker tap tapping away
in his brain.

At three I push Tom's arms
into his man sized coat, grab
the bread I've cut into one centimetre
cubes and we head for the bridge
to throw the bread in the water.
Feeding ducks quietens
the quacks in my son's mind.

Then it's wildlife programmes on TV
with his tea on his knees
while I do chores. Then bed. Tom
sleeps from nine till five, when
the cry of a seagull wakes him,
and they both come down the stairs
wanting herrings for breakfast.

Susan Jane Sims

Bird Daughter

Her father flies off the handle
when I call our daughter a bird.

I carry on and sew her wings
with invisible thread,

work each stitch by starlight
through my magnifying glass,

give her my heart as though it's a violin,
the strings tuned to breaking point.

I show her the night owl in me
wooing her to the tops of trees.

My daughter must learn
all she can taste from the wind.

Jo Roach

L'Inconnue De La Seine

There was a swell on the surface of the Seine that day
making faces at me. So I blew kisses at an open mouth

and whispered, "Drown me peaceful, drown me slow."
I wanted the time, you see, to float undead through Paris.

I could have choked on a glass of milk as a child
and missed this opportunity. Don't call it suicide

as if it's a tragedy. This was the first time in my life
I had been in control of anything. Imagine, not dying

but dissolving, becoming a river. Was I afraid?
Not of the fall. I was afraid of the Water Police,

the way they walk along the river, any one of them
could have seen me floating, but nightfall saved me.

Before the river had me, I had one last look at the stars
"Just look at you," I said, "already dead and still shining."

Seni Seneviratne

The Boy Who Loved Birds

i.m. H. F.

My brother died in a dismal rented flat.
Last summer in the city's stuffy heat
his heart broke and he died there quite alone,
watched by a barn owl and the starkest porn.
He'd disappeared, thought to be moving house,
his precious things in store, just that glass case
to keep the past with him. That eager boy,
obsessed with birds, had seen one summer day
the half-crown owl among the bric-a-brac,
bought it, opposed by all, a good day's work.

The phone that rang and rang – 'He's moving house'
we said with truth, and now I say 'Oh please
can birds, not angels swoop his new abode?'
That kind and funny man, he can't be dead.
What use his wit, his learning, wasted on
winged po-faced angels with no use for wine.
Danger he loved, would risk the wild and rough;
to bring our mother eggs braved dizzy cliff,
despite the sharp-beaked gulls, sea far below.
Her death made him more fragile than we knew.

In an old-fashioned bird book we once read:
'Swifts scream exultantly', and commented
on anthropomorphism and new research.
In headlong flight swifts scream to keep in touch
it seems. Our radar failed; he won't return.
The swifts, they'll soon race overhead again;
their switchback glory ride, their blue-black gleam,
their arrogance and mystery, scream his name.
I dread their cries. They'll tell of death, alone,
a week dead with his owl and that shrill phone.

Jo Peters

84

In the Garden

Yesterday my son was in the garden.
He was beautiful in green,
but didn't speak.

I began to mutter,
Do you have a coat? A torch?
Will you be all right in the dark?

He turned away,
walked swiftly, past the gunnera
towards the sea.

Today I can't find him.
Death is hovering
in the cafe.

We talk about my son.
I look Death straight
in the hollows of his skull.

My son is in the garden
wearing green.
He's not ready. Let him be.

He's out of sight amongst the trees
but I know my son is in the garden
wearing green.

Jenny Hamlett

whenever the van pulls up

For weeks my father thrashed the animal
to make it heel –
unruly dogs must be broken.

Aunt Irene often told us how their old man
took a belt to his son,
who then enlisted at sixteen

as soon as war broke out.
The ghost of a whipped boy
walked the house of my father.

My mother, pleading with him to stop,
slowly conceded to the mercy
of having the creature put down.

But still, years later, that van pulls up:
she makes a soundless lurch towards the rap at the door

and the boxer quivers, his coat rippling sheeny
as before a beating.

My father has already left for work
so my mother is alone when

the stricken eyes beg
one last time for reprieve ...

Then the van drives off.

On this mid June morning,
a breeze lapping in from the sea
she doesn't go for a walk.

Linda Rose Parkes

Pray

*Pray for Aurelia. She has a court case pending
and she misses her children.* (Prayer Request, Church of Our Lady)

Pray for her.
For God has made her in his own image.
For this image startles her as she passes a shop window.
For she sees a cardigan (sleeves unravelling),
skirt (waist tied with string). Odd socks.
For the name-tag on her coat says *Melanie.*
For she knows God will clothe her. She's a *lily of the field.*
For she has no thoughts of tomorrow.

Sufficient unto the day is the evil thereof

She's fat with drugs. They've stuffed and stuffed her.
She has no teeth.
Her children have been taken from her.

Pray for her.
For she has a first class degree but her mind has betrayed her.
For betrayal is the only thing she knows.
For her father lifts his grand-daughter onto the swing in the local park,
touching her ever so, ever so gently.

For her mother didn't listen.
Nor her brother, her sister, her teacher, her lover.

She's a loony.
She's a swing door.
She's a bin-liner.

Pray for her.
For God has made her in his own image.
For he is with her even through *the valley of the shadow of death*

Which is her life, you know. Her one and only. Life.

Vivienne Tregenza

Cicatrice

spreading her legs
the labia minora
opened like a bud

the clitoris
is easy to excise
a penknife will do it

roughen the inner edges
of the labia majora
tie her knees and thighs

haemorrhage   shock
septicaemia   fever

types I to III in pictures
document how much is altered
how much cut
and what is sewn   with gut or thorn
or held abraded till the scar
can form

how tissue thin it is
at first
the female element
how dangerous

urinary and rectal fistula

on a dirt floor or in a doctor's offices
woman to woman
down the matrilineal line
these secret lacerations

type IV (not pictured)
gathers all the rest
like pricking of the clitoris
with pins or narrowing the opening
with herbs or other harmful substances

one hundred million women
three million girls each year

infertility   still birth

"they pulled my legs apart"
"four strong women
held me down"

and I'm reminded how we used to go
into the pen at home
I'd hold a six week calf against the wall and he
with burning iron
would press against the growing tips of horn
disbudding them

cysts   abscesses   open wounds

her monthly blood backs up
and exits drop by drop

when asked she says her urine flow is
"normal"
the question is rephrased – how long to urinate?
"15 minutes, normal"
is what she says

pelvic infections   UTI

then there's the second cut

her husband on their wedding night
must cut her to consume
to consummate

vaginal closure   painful intercourse

her husband goes to war
her husband's mother sews her smaller
keeps her pure

acute urinary retention
prolonged obstructed labour

one hundred million women
three million girls each year

Janet Sutherland

The Devil finds work for idle hands

my father said. I was reading,
so didn't reply, but used my hands
to turn the pages. His hands hovered
around his pipe. Would the Devil
flame out of the bowl? But only
puffs of smoke emerged. Was my father
signalling to passing Red Indians,
begging them to carry me off
to be a squaw? But then he sighed,
meaning there was nothing to be done,
but he wasn't to blame
that I wasn't the expected son,
and what's more, showed no womanly qualities,
only laying the table when asked
with an air of put-upon martyrdom.

Daphne Schiller

Kid Gloves

Put up your dukes he chortles fists
clenched feinting

Dad's happy again got a new job
keep moving he yells

Watch your feet Sugar Ray would win
by dancing

You know I was semi pro once he tells her
on a tramp steamer   sailed

the world He was good kept his guard
up tells her to do the same

Now she's bunched up   wards off blows,
hears herself shriek   wonders

why he doesn't see her tears but thinks
it beats the tickling

when she's fending off his fingers when
the gloves are off

Wendy Klein

A Tray of Frozen Songbirds

For our last meal together
my father takes out of the freezer
a tray of frozen songbirds.
He's saved them up, these delicacies
with ice crystals in their beaks,
wings stuck to ribcages.
There are skylarks, blackbirds, doves.
He tells me how some were plucked
while still alive,
about the mist net at dawn,
how one nightingale was thrust
into a sack of discarded heads
and cried, then the poacher licked
the sticky lime from its plumes
tenderly, before slitting its throat.
He pours champagne as if it's
the river of life.
We eat like two drunks
woken from dreams of flying,
me on his lap, singing the song
I've just learnt at school – *Alouette,*
gentille alouette, alouette, je te plumerai.

Pascale Petit

The Knowing

The story goes that the light slipped past/and entered the room like a shout/he stood over me/a woodcutter entered the forest/and the trees began to warn each other/it was July or maybe June/the knowing settled at my throat/a clever raven/it never left/does not believe in trees or flying/the light slipping past/it is sometimes painful/to have a knowing at your throat/that clever raven/but better than the alternative/something small and bruised/the raven knows most things/it remembers nothing/ this is really about the trees/which saw it all.

Kim Moore

Buckle

He drove her to Seaford once, so drunk
she stripped off and swam out
into the black sea, sea wall
smaller and smaller, until she
was just a dot.

Other teenagers he'd filled his car with
spilled out along the dark
beach, necking red wine,
and screaming like seagulls, until
even that stopped.

Charlotte Gann

Watching my mother turn into a wasp

Tiny and yellow, suddenly furious –
she settles on the chair, clutches her bag,
and rages; but her voice is muffled, small,

as if under glass. We watch her
scrabbling to get at us, angry with the world.
Nobody nobody cares. She's terrified.

She will not eat. She says *oh let me die*
and then *I hate it here.* Whispers her rosary,
the first few words, droning from half closed lips
HolymarymotherofGod, take me Jesus....
The eyes are small and black, unfocussed,
inward turned, seeing the terrible future,

the threatening shadows moving beyond reach.
She brushes off my hand. In her mind,
she hurls herself against unyielding glass,

to find a crack, a gap, a clean escape,
something, anything, half alive to sting.

Ann Alexander

Blackbird

When they locked me
in the cellar

and told me to count
slowly to a hundred,

each number
became a blackbird's feather

and all the darkness
sang

through the keyhole
of my yellow beak.

Pascale Petit

To My Husband

Why were your tears so few
when your mother died?
You loved her, I know,
but years ago
she ripped the fabric of your life.

She tried, she told me, many times
to make it good.
Maybe the needle was blunt
or the thread kept breaking.

Poor, bewildered little boy:
long years ago your tears were shed
when you were sent away
to that strange safety far from home.
'He's not all there,' the strangers said.

Your mother told me this,
tears in her eyes.
'Don't let him down,' she said.

Jackie Hinden

Silence

I remember saying: I think I'll wash my hair.
It's 10 at night, you'll catch your death!
I remember crying over the basin
until my eyes were red,
the knowing look she gave me
when I blamed it on shampoo.
I remember how we hugged,
how I felt her body shake with sobs.
I remember watching
as his silence spread around the house
like hoar frost in the garden,
and I remember how we waited
for a thaw that never came.

Margaret Beston

My Father's Life in a Glass Coffin

I am turned back on myself by your invisible walls,
again and again like a bird I have stunned myself against you.

I might batter my way in with a brick, cut entry with a diamond,
but I am not strong or skilled enough.

And you, would you shrivel in air?

We are both shaped (you inside, me out)
by this distorting mirror.

Your eyes ice-blue as weathered glaciers
behind defensive glasses –

surely the right word would have thawed you free,
that word neither of us could say.

But you were young once, molten and incandescent,
the heat of your youth sparked my beginning.

Now you are old and cooled. And in the fire
of your final smelting, shall I be re-forged?

Joanna Boulter

My Father's Mother

When I think of her I see smoke
looping from the ashtray
like a silver-white spring giving up its bounce, I see crime novels
piled by the bedside and although I was not there,
I see the scene she recounted to my mother in hushed tones
many weeks after the fact – my grandfather
pouring hot tea in her lap.
                    When I think of her I hear
the plaintive tune of that soap opera she clung to –
still, I cannot bear the sound – I hear
the premature rasp in her voice and the yap
of that infernal dog and most of all I hear
silence, canyons in the things she said
like the night my mother brought me, an infant,
to her house after my father beat her
and my grandmother said, yes she said it –
in my day when you made your bed you lay in it.
I can tell you there is none of the woman I knew
in that statement, there is
bitterness and echoes
of what she must have been told
in her youth
you make your bed, you lie in it –
a hinge, a tidal force, a false gravity
that made her marry him, forgive him, endure him,
even when he lifted the hot cup and poured it,
poured it all
in my grandmother's lap.

Carolyn Jess-Cooke

Honeysuckle Sides

When you half-rouse at two or three, burrow back quickly into the fug of sleep.
If your fingers smooth the pillowcase, do not remember the crispness of the
                                                                    notes
you counted three times to be sure he had filched one from your purse.

Push away the image of dull eyes evading yours; his stubble, matted hair
and the sour smell of him at breakfast. Do not recall that thump in the guts
when you broke his ban, tidied his room and found the syringe under dirty
                                                                    clothes

because then you will have to slide out of bed, put on your dressing gown, turn
the door handle very quietly and end up in the kitchen putting another teabag
into your William Morris mug, warming your hands on its honeysuckle sides
while your feet become almost as cold as his in a doorway or cardboard box.

Jean Watkins

My Daughter

Every few weeks she'll drop by
to throw a brick through the window
or set fire to the gate again.

The last time she entered the house
it was with a protective hand
held up against her face the entire stay.

She was here ten minutes then
gone into the ever shortening light.
Sometimes I'll be on the bus

and she'll be cycling like mad
down the other side of the road
dangerously close to a lorry.

I waved once. She never sees me.
When I'm brushing up the glass
after the latest attack

occasionally I'll notice her
watching from the corner
of the street. I can't really tell

but I think she's got thinner.
The year I turned up at her school
everyone went quiet when I walked in:

no one would say how she was doing.
I try to imagine her bedroom:
the pattern on her duvet

what posters she's got on the walls
the mess on the floor, whether
she's kept anything from before

which way she sleeps.
Someone said they lock the doors
at night, just in case

but she always goes back
even though she could leave
even though I've said.

Rosie Miles

Sub Title: A Visual Exploration of Fetish

Sunny Girl's hollering through the letterbox.
It's my birthday. I follow the tail
of her Davy Crockett hat down the hall.
She hands me a glossy hardback:
Doris Kloster's *Demimonde*

'Quick! Look inside. There's a picture of you.'
I locate a dog-eared page and peer.
'It's not *me*.'
'Yes it is. What's up? Don't you like it?'
My head nods. My mouth smiles.
She kisses my hand and scoots.

I show Ted.
The woman in question is coupled
in a game of female bondage.
She's wearing red ankle boots and a thong.
He's impressed.
'Well ... she *does* look a bit like you,
apart from that rose tattoo on her cheek ...'

He returns to his Sunday paper.
I pore over the rest of the book.
On the centrefold there's an oldish man
in a leather pouch, all wrapped up in cling film.
In his mouth's an orange.

'I see the government's advocating free allotments
for the over fifties ...'
'It's not normal,' I say.

Maggie Sawkins

Recovery Stroke

How heavy it seems, this duck in flight,
wing down and flattened, not knowing

if it will have the strength to pull up again
waiting for the next push forwards,

a divine acrobat, comical at times,
stuck on the wall in threes

as if there is something quite absurd,
ridiculous, about a duck in flight,

but look at its beauty:
every feather and tendon

used to the maximum in its rotation
of back and forth, up and down,

knowing without being told
that moving forward

requires a moving back,
that no stroke is wasted

that the greatest beauty sometimes
happens at the weakest point.

Rosie Jackson

Strangers

Don't count on me I'm just a loser
I can't be your guiding star
Never could refuse your love or choose it
I'm a stranger here, as you are
For every question there's ten answers
And then a hundred questions more
Fortune never smiles, she merely glances
You're not the only one she's looking for
> We're lost, without a rhyme or a reason
> Leaves shaken off a tree
> Lost, it's the human condition
> What you get is what you see
> Don't go blaming me
> When you're lost you're free

Sat down with a shrink in Tobermory
Listened to a preacher on Capri
Dressed in different clothes the same old story
Don't think too much, just follow me
For every fact there's twenty fictions
For every truth a hundred lies
And if you spot the contradictions
You're not welcome in their paradise
We're lost, without a song or a season
> Loose stones rolling down the scree
> Lost, it's a slippery position
> We might not be home for tea
> Don't go blaming me
> When you're lost you're free

Don't count on me, I'm just a minstrel
And I can't read the notes you write
Nothing can be sung, unless it sings well
Here is no scented rose, no pale moonlight
For every chord there's ten inversions
For every tune, it's counterpart
With every take, the soundtrack worsens
There are no verses left to learn by heart
> We're lost, without a might or a maybe
> Off the piste without a ski
> Lost and it's, *Who loves you baby?*
> Not a soul that I can see
> Don't go blaming me
> When you're lost you're free

Bumped into a broker in Milwaukee
Heard a politician make a speech
Everything they said conspired to bore me
Those weasel words of diplomacy
For every deal a devastation
For every prince ten million poor
And if you rise above your station
You won't remember where you lived before
    We're lost, without a fund or a fashion
    In Berkeley Square without a key
    Lost, not a pavement to crash on
    In the throes of bankruptcy
    Don't go blaming me
    When you're lost you're free

Don't count on me, I'm just a loner
I can't be your helping hand
Everything you touch, you want to own it
There's nothing left my friend, no promised land
For every god there's fifty faces
For every faith a hundred more
Half a billion stars just died in space as
We turned the lights down low and closed the door
    We're lost, without a moon or a mission
    A beach ball floating out to sea
    Lost, on a doomed expedition
    It's the only place to be
    Ride the waves with me
    Ah, can't you see
    We're lost, we're lost, we're lost – we're free

Hylda Sims

editors' note: *Strangers* is originally published as a song.
Musical notation is included in the collection in which it appears:
p44/45, *Sayling the Babel* (Hearing Eye)

Ablutions

I've chosen Bach's cello suites, the Casals
and opened the window above the bath.
For the first time in months, a kind of faith
rises in me, like the slow hoist of sails
or a semiquaver's climb through intervals
up the ledger-line ladder of its staff.
It's not a game of blindfold in the dark –
it's like learning to see again with braille.
It's my still-warm pyjamas in a pile
on the floor; how I slip myself in, toe-
first. The way, in water, the body drifts,
forgets itself sometimes, travels miles
and how the pulse this heart emits, although
submerged, will sound the body home. It's this.

Michaela Ridgway

Section 3:   LOVE VARIATIONS

Indwelling

A woman holds the head of a man
in her lap, brother, husband,
friend or lover,
asleep on a bench

and I long to hold the shape of a nest
in my hands.

Someone, with nowhere else to sleep,
has built a shelter
from fallen branches

in this glade of bluebells, so blue,
it seems infinite.

Sharon Morris

from *Gospel Oak*, Enitharmon Press, 2013

Garnet for Birth

In January you bought me a birthstone ring.
I read how warriors going to battle
might, for luck, carry a garnet
to stop the losing of blood.

Such evocative names for a stone:
mandarin, pyrope, almandine –
for me they evoke Merovingian gold
and one sad queen who lies alone
in a Frankish tomb with a garnet ring
translucent as seeds of the bright
pomegranate – that fertile
abundant fruit...

Today the sky is nursery blue.
Garnets come in every shade, except for blue.
You mutter words of re-assurance
tuck my sheet in, squeeze my hand;
I rest the garnet on my belly,
pray it stops the blood.

Mandy Pannett

Never so much as larva

This miniature raincoat in *Stop!* red,
black spots on cuffs and collar,
the giant ladybird pocket –
I see her running through puddles,
mud-spatter on her bare legs;
I hear her shapeless coat squeak
with every jump and swoop.
Now she's huddled on the doorstep,
straining to steady her hand
as she paints dot after dot
onto red wellington boots.
Her brilliance from such a distance
stuns me. And as I reach out
my finger to touch this happy coat
on its peg, I almost laugh but
it still makes no sense that I miss
the daughter who was never
so much as larva or egg within me,
and all I can do at this moment
is bolt home to write her alive.

Anne Ryland

Silent Daughter

In my mind, she's a summer one,
folded away like linen,
facing in.

At times, the thinnest moon
is her tiny seashell, clipping
in a pea green sky.

See, she's a whisper of wool;
an empty swing swinging
in a big hay barn.

In my mind, she meanders
round the rose garden,
her fingers lingering

on petal tips of pink and lemon,
even milk teeth
of thorn.

Just once we touched:
a butterfly kiss of lids grown thick
with longing.

But I was still a child myself,
too slight to bear
the brunt of her.

Charlotte Gann

Rose Petals

Opening the wardrobe door, I am met again
by the blurred scent of rose petals and skin
My clothes hang limp as the dead
and one fine pleated shirt, bone colour, stands out
formal as a shroud.

When do we see them now, the sheeted dead?
They go out of the back door with the men in black
without the viewing and wake
without the lilies and candles at foot and head
and the ceremonial cake

I remember her in her nightgown, one day old
I touch the mirror glass of the door   She wasn't cold
the July child, but half warm
like an egg not long laid
like a small fallen plum in the long grass and deep shade

Nor was she marble white but a waxy grey
the rosebud put in her fingers gone flat and blue
The loss of a sister can never be put away
I shut the boxwood door, but without relief
from the death of the child who taught my childhood grief

Ann Phillips

Cord

On the fifth day I find it in your cot –
still held firm in a plastic clip.

When the nurse lay you on my chest
it pulsed between us, blue-white

vigorous, the best I had to give –
stem-cell, lymphocytes, streaming

down the line they had to cut off.
Nine months of nurture you shed

easy as a snake discards its skin.
All that remains, here, in my palm –

a twist of ochre, a swirl of red,
a swell of black like a fossilised eye

opaque with remembering.
I hoard it in a matchbox as I would

a snail shell, the hook of a cocoon,
a milk tooth, a curl.

Victoria Gatehouse

Che Angelo

An angel is
as this toddler is, on the Vaporetto,
sunk into his mother's body,
chin on her breast

        so still
an occasional shudder
in his shoulders.

We stare
as we chug down the Grand Canal.
Approaching Rialto,
someone whispers *che angelo*.

The mother's held, her breath slowed;
no oil-on-canvas putto, the child
        spills into her
as when a flame spurts, licks,
the hot top invisible.

Jane Kirwan

Past the Rose Hips

to Sebastian, at 17 months

Clink and clatter in the kitchen,
                    then it's hiding
            behind you. Outside,
the worn stone steps, cool and smooth,
                    are falling below.
You don't want to fall.
                    You hold your arms up so
            Ammi will carry you down.
Each step jumps out but you are both safe. She
                    stands you up beyond the prickly pebbles
    that will bite your bare feet.
Now you're plodding over the easy grass
                    never looking round.
                    You go faster and faster.
You pass shiny round red hips like hard little apples
                    but you twice tried them –
                    they are no good...
You reach another part of the garden.
                    Your feet remember
            the other small red ones...
they shine between these leaves.
                    So many good things are red.
            You will pull them off
                    one by one.
            They are like little hats
                    that fit your fingers.
You know them.
                    They taste sweet.
                    You do not know how to say
    their name is raspberries

Melinda Lovell

Arlo's Song

this is my bed and this is my sofa and this
is my staircase and this is my this and this is
my table and this is my chair and this is my
bathroom and this is my flannel and this
is my cream

       two year old conducting his
dad round their house singing his ABC
and counting to fifteen and jumping and
rubbing his chest where the boiling coffee
lifted his skin though it won't leave a scar
they promise

Janet Fisher

Scarp Song

My two strong sons skate out in one small shoe
    treading the polished water
across inverted hills that hang stone heads
among the white clouds in its green glass mirror.

The wind sleeps, and a blanket mist may thicken,
    hiding the polished water,
and no one knows which breathing wind may cloud
the glass, and frost or shiver the green mirror.

All my love's work sits in that far white boat,
    trusting the smiling traitor,
diminishes beyond duststorms of birds.
I see long threads of white hair in the mirror.

My sons ride fearlessly, far out to sea;
    I would not have them other:
they cheat the traitor of his mackerel shoal
and teach the lobster to repent his error.

Northeaster, chase them home; bring rainbow weather
    across the ruffled water.
Confine, Southwest, remorseless water-walls
that travel blind. I dare not name my terror.

Anna Adams

Dandelion Time

We have only the photograph
to remember the exact shape
of his mouth, his concentration

as he bent to pull at the ground,
turned to blow in slow deliberation
oblivious to the pointing camera.

We smooth his pale round face,
tracing the outline as he puffs
each weightless hour away.

Some years later he grabs at a stalk,
running as he blows, tossing the clock
away in his haste to keep moving.

Alison Hill

Cotton Thread

Here you are, sauntering from the park,
waving goodbye to your friend at the corner,
checking your tight, black curls in the newsagent's window,
back to my cottage where you will show me a loose cotton thread
on your High School Musical T-shirt. You pull it.
No! I say, *It'll fall apart.*
You giggle, share the thread with me – *Pull it, Nan.*
And I do. And we laugh as a whole seam unravels.

You and I holding a thread so easily broken –
there you are, wearing a crimson headscarf, carrying
a big blue bowl of mangoes on your head, strong
legs rolling beneath you, arms pushing you on
down a white dusty road, brown eyes fixed
on another grandmother's home.

Marilyn Ricci

Face to Face

My father, eighty four, shaves himself
slowly and calmly
without tremor
in front of a slightly mottled bathroom mirror
round and familiar
as a London Transport sign

It is a soothing ritual,
he rarely nicks himself
with his ancient kit –
no need to change it,
this razor is perfectly adequate,
this little wooden handled brush a treat

When I was seven maybe – if that –
I used to become absorbed, intently
watching him. Pyjama clad,
using that dinky shaving brush
he'd cover chin and cheeks with lather
and then I'd wait patiently
for cheeks and chin to come back,
the razor rather like a snow plough
accumulating drifts
to be sloughed off in lukewarm water
a few economic inches
in a Shanks basin

I was joining in
with my father's reflection first thing
and if his eyes smiled
those crinkly lines I liked
collected at their far corners.
It was all right to be there
hearing birdsong and steam train
but no words said
and my small owl gaze
not in any way minded

Melinda Lovell

April 10th, 1929

I am four today.
Father holds my hand,
we walk – my birthday treat –

to a nearby wood
and there in whispers
he points out Red Riding Hood.

I see her still, a basket on her arm,
cloak poppy-red and by a tree
a hairy face, teeth bared.

I see them both and chestnut trees,
father's arms and safety.
I have no memory of his face

at thirty-one,
twenty years younger
than my youngest son.

Bernie Kenny

A Day at the Seaside

I didn't see it until I trod
on a broken piece and screamed,
as much from the sight of all that
welling redness which spurted
over golden sand and stained it
as from any pain I felt.

Dad turned and grabbed me,
had the glass out in seconds;
a cursory wipe with his hand
then his hankie, its soft warmth
like balm across my skin.
Then he sucked the cut clean,
bound it tight

and before I had time to cry
swung me high on his shoulders,
whistling. I like to think
there might have been promises
of ice cream at the pier. The grown-ups,
momentarily disturbed,
walked on across the beach.

Shirley Wright

February 27

Leaning down to a flower shaken by a bee,
leaning so low that petals vibrate
on your cheek (an eyelash kiss
forgotten since childhood – a mother's eye

close to your own, tender and silly,
trying to see what you see), you might
imagine why, from a house in mourning,
someone could well step out, bend low

to just such a shaking flower, where seeds
start in a hum of wings, mere words
vibrating too, more song than thought.
Breathing a welcome to what may come.

After all, this bee will have crossed strange ground,
traced a faint scent on a chill wind,
the sun warm enough, at long last, for wings
though, not far off, the snow is falling.

Anne Cluysenaar

Zeno's Playground

Mother is at one end of the lot, clapping,
shouting encouragement to a child on a bicycle –
a wavering bicycle not taking the straightest path.
The child advances first a yard, then half a yard,
then half that half, then half that distance,
trying, but never quite making it to mother
who stands at the other side, forever.

Lara Frankena

Kiss

It was done only in public –
at airports, at the foot of gang-ways
when I was leaving or coming home.

No air-kissing either, but honest lip to lip,
lip to cheek, plosive contact
and *Safe Journey* or *Welcome back.*

My two-dimensional parents
– the background I drew on –
never said that they loved me.

They smiled from the sideboard
in black-and-white battle and wedding dress,
steadily outflanked by school

and graduation photographs. I moved away.
Phoned my messages. *Merry Christmas.*
Happy Birthday. See you soon.

And I miss them. I hug close
my hand-knitted childhood,
my unkissed parents

and their faith in me.

Laurna Robertson

Mudlark

A curlew's feather, mackerel-marked, blew
towards the dark shore of Kent. We all turned
as one, seeing the channel cut for the cockle-boats
filling up fast.

'Don't cross the creek'
but we always did – skirts tucked up
joining the pale-legged boys, ration-book thin.

I don't recall fear –
just knew we'd better get across now, slip into
warm water, wade to the bank
pull the little ones out.

A sinister geography enters my dreams.
I'm alone in rough tides,
between the two shores,
not knowing which one is nearer, which one to head for.

Last night you were with me, swimming behind me,
cupping my thighs, setting me right
with a life-saving bottle-nosed nudge.

Ann Segrave

Letter from my Brother

When I saw those words a goose flew into my chest
and beat its wings in there, and there was laughing

on the other side, where all the chickens, the litters,
were scrambling up the sides and down, on the grass,

falling over each other in their innocence. Fresh-daisy
excitement! The sun beating down on our heads,

the laughing, the beach huts, the long promenade
with the huge round pebbles below, the wind, the light-

grey of the sea wall and the suck of that wind, pulling
our faces into smiles, smiling itself; the stripes, awning,

rain – and always the laughter, incessant, long—ours.
Our show, our imagined world, the singing, chancing,

and everywhere the awning. We were stiff as frost,
folded, stacked, but the breath on the glass was ours.

Kay Syrad

When you dream stone, I dream water...

whether in Clahane slipping on seaweed
that slicks limestone pavements

or watching you hunkered over stones
on the beach as you look for jewels,

deciphering carnelian, amber,
agate, hidden among shingle,

as I swim in chill water, currents
tugging me towards rough rocks.

I long to reach your stony shore,
where you wrap me in dry towels,

rub my shoulders, hold me
in a deep, warm hug.

Rosy Wilson

The Photograph

A young woman's outstretched hand,
small for an adult, nails hard bitten down,
held out toward a window on some stairs,
on it a butterfly, brown as the old jumper sleeve
just in frame, unravelling round a slim wrist.
Some foliage. A sunny day.

My daughter's on the landing, half-way up
or down, gathering essentials from her room,
readying to leave home for the first time.
I know she's happy to be going away
and scared. I know I'm happy for her,
glad she's letting me help load the van
to take her to the new life; and sad.
I know I'm trying not to say.

And then the butterfly.

At first it fluttered at the pane, struggling
to find a way out to the sun, confused perhaps
by the over-grown house-plant on the sill,
but when my daughter reached out her hand,
it came to her and seemed to settle, long enough
for me to fetch the camera, steady my hand,
capture the brief alighting before it flew away.

Lorna Dexter

Leaving home

Last night your absence woke me.
No gentle breath, no stirrings from your room.

Standing in moonlight, I watched
your empty bed, and felt the cord

stretch taut between us. Like a climber
you test the edges of your world,

harnessed by love.
Once I could haul you back.

Helen Jagger

Crossbar

Emotions budded then like tender breasts,
her child's certainty giving way to doubt.
Her chatter became shy, all the 11 plus
cleverness failed. Not yet 13 she was hatched
but not steady, on the cusp. He took her up,
an older boy, set her on his crossbar.
She could not learn her body's new behaviour –
why whispers in her hair brought tears near,
the brush of a bare arm made her shiver,
hands warm through the damp of her swimsuit
melted her belly, like fear.
As if she were still the child she couldn't be,
he dropped her for an older girl. Heartbreak
was easy to learn, that first grown-up hurt.

Cynthia Fuller

Remembering Daffodils

An Earl's Court room, an unpoetic place
and you arrived with daffodils
bought at the Tube.

Clean-stemmed in their glass jar
they shone against the peeling paint;
"These flowers, what are they called?"
you asked in careful English.

Told, you laughed, remembering your English class,
and later, as you lay beside me in our rumpled bed,
intoned: "Oh, daffodils, we weep to see
you haste away so soon..."

And laughed again, with me,
to think that poems flower on,
out-lasting red-inked maps.

I wonder if, a world away,
you still remember me,
and quoting Herrick's daffodils?

Val Doyle

The Discovery

Warm scent of rain, yourself at the open door,
eager for the morning, rain-blessed,
this baptism of being in love, the respite.

Rain the colour of metal, rain in midgey fleets,
rain softer than the padding of cats,
warm scent of rain, yourself at the open door.

Risen from the bed, fresh-bread smell of sheets,
the breakfast ceremony of croissants,
this baptism of being in love, the respite.

The dead drone of rain, the cheerlessness,
yet today in July loneliness,
warm scent of rain, yourself at the open door.

There's nothing here but discovery,
what made everything shine was rain,
this baptism of being in love, the respite.

Rain is the happiness of lovers in the rain,
all of it embroidered with rain,
warm scent of rain, yourself at the open door,
this baptism of being in love, the respite.

S J Litherland

Without Resolution

You draw a diagram connecting moon and earth
and with black ink, score in radiating lines.
You mark the ratio of circle to diameter,
add some smaller globes, a shadowed sun.

Disturbingly, you give the moon a blurred circumference,
insist on the beauty of pi,
                                 confusing me with formulae
that are fixed and infinite. Certainty has hooks.

We share a sun and moon.
We do not share a common speech.
I do not know your words for wax and wane.

The lines are hard as arrows to a bull. Planets
you have strewn like bubbles, balls that shimmer.
There's an equation for surface tension
that says why rainbows so reflected, shiver, settle, vanish.

Jane Kirwan

Ripened

You had left me, gone up to bed.
I went outside to see the changed pattern
of the moon. A cloud hung against the sky.
The stars had changed, their positions moved.

It was the time of the autumn equinox,
of movement, of ripeness, when emotions
are gathered with the fruit to savour
through the cold until
we, like the trees, are covered by frost.

Carolyn O'Connell

Second Anniversary

On that April day,
we and the clouds were contained
in whiteness.

You had to point out
the cotton-reel on the windowsill,
thread inviting me out of the frame
and into the garden
where the trail unfolded.

I uncovered a handkerchief
tucked in a shell; two place mats;
a T-shirt making a statement –
a size too small,
a tiny coverlet, just right.

And we turned and laughed,
embracing as near as we could
over the lurch of a baby
quite delicate
in delaying its coming,

or perhaps wanting its own anniversary
to be distinct.

All I knew was that cotton
would be good next to new skin,
and I trusted to leather sinews
of the next anniversary
to keep the third one safe.

Of that cotton day
what I remember is whiteness
unwilling to task us.

Belinda Singleton

Glacier-Walk

Jostedalsbreen, Norway

We tread on a dome of locked light,
a thousand stars in a winter shield.

Our bones have budded iron –
ice-picks from fists, crampons from feet.
Our hearts quicken as if we are hares.

I lead but you are anchor, ready to weigh
if I fall. Not much rope for a marriage,
perhaps, six metres spanning between us

as we test out our steps on the ice.
If I walk too fast, you drag me back –
too slow, and I might trip you –

small details for such dazzle,
these sapphires shaping round us,
crisp with firn. We edge along, cervine

and inch back from crevasses in our minds,
old cracks of grief where love
might fall or all the stars wink out.

Lynne Wycherley

Nightscape

You came and picked me up at two a.m.
without me asking. What was in your mind?
That danger might be walking home with me
this night more than the other hundred times?

I've often told you how I love the air
at two a.m. when it's so clear and clean
the nightbirds' warnings not to interfere
seem to include me in their reach of care.

Or how the moon slides her shy way
behind a wisp of cloud and sends a flood
of ash-grey light, a one-night only show
that's just for me, played on the shining road.

You enter, centre stage, and change the scene.
We talk a little. But not of air or moon.

Anne Stewart

Husband Sewing

The whirr of the machine
under your hands,
first snow skating down
the window to melt
on the ledge.
These are lean years
when things must last.
The threads have learnt to flow
from your fingers.
What lurks beyond your gift
for mending,
the hum of your gaze
along silk edges
of intimate seam,
double stitching?
When I put on this coat
I may want to undress you,
wear the climate
of shared skin.

Linda Rose Parkes

An Afternoon

My nose is nervous, but the flannelette sheets
smell of talc; he's emptied lavender
over them and the pillows.

The mattress rolls us together like a gigantic
breaker; we struggle in its breathless trough.
He's cleaned his teeth,

taken a bath: *Anything for my darling.*
Clocks tick on the table, on the wall,
as if he's not afraid of time.

Born too late for one war, too old for the next,
bullets are less real to him than raindrops.
Still are; the planet's wars

are a fantasy, like books, like plays
he can't be doing with. This is real;
the village, the street,

the fields, the woods, the animals, the gossip,
and going to bed without clothes, a novelty
he's making the most of.

His skin is tough, his arms determined,
and his bum is rounded and hard,
unlike the old man –

too long without use, until persuasion
stiffens the sinews. When his family call,
loving and kind,

he dwindles to Dad-in-the-corner,
but now he's the merry ploughboy
with an eye for the women.

Joan Downar

Daisy

I met you online and
our relationship could be described
as friendship plus...
but you love
my aged border collie.
You found a cardboard sign
on a washing powder packet, with her name
in bright letters.
It is for the door of the cupboard
where she goes to sleep,
and, as I push the drawing pin in,
I know that one day
I will be taking it off.
Will I be sadder
that the dog is dead
or that I don't see you anymore?
Though we've been apart three days now
and I ache for you,
I think the dog will have the edge.

Jo Peters

You, Lizard-like

expert at loss, loyal to none,
slip into unknown spaces, claws
digging quickly in, out. You disappear
between things and survive.

Can never go back yet alter course;
are a foreigner in your own company,
who can fade into the dimness of a room
and still be there. Dutiful to darkness.

You hear and seek, see and hide.
Light colours your inner world
as the outer one changes. How quickly
you can flee and shed your skin.

Innocently unfaithful to mate or nest.

Lynne Hjelmgaard

And

Sex is like Criccieth. You thought it would be
a tumble of houses into a pure sea
and so it must have been, in eighteen-ten.
The ranks of boarding houses marched up then.
They linger, plastic curtains at their doors,
or, still more oddly, blonde ungainly statues.
The traffic swills along the single street
and floods the ears, until our feet
turn down towards the only shop for chips,
to shuffling queues, until sun slips
behind the Castle, which must be, by luck,
one of the few a Welsh prince ever took.
Or in the café, smoked with fat, you wait.
Will dolphins strike the sea's skin? They do not.

And yet, a giant sun nobody has told
of long decline, beats the rough sea to gold.
The Castle rears up with its tattered flag,
hand laces hand, away from valleys' slag.
And through the night, the long sea's dolphined breath
whispers into your warm ear, 'Criccieth'.

Alison Brackenbury

Syszygy

Moonlight on the Schuylkyll,
we take things slow, driving in
downtown past rows
of crumbling clapboard houses
to Alma da Cuba, way up
Walnut Street between South 16th
and 17th, parking so easy
it seems like a good omen

but it's wild there: dark,
cool cocktails, guapo waiters,
and that hot Cuban beat
of rockason. We're hungry,
gorge our way through Gloria's
black bean soup, Pulpo con
Causa, Big Eye Tuna, and all
of these just for starters, Olé .

Then it's Vaca Frita for me,
Papas Huancaina for Jake,
Oysters Rodriguez for Max –
so far, so good, but soon
the rot sets and we have
this crazy competition,
downing Mojitos El Jefe,
matching glass for glass.

Hombre! I'm in their king-size,
no sign of clothes or keys,
You guys are meant to be gay,
I yell, torn between guilt
and pleasure as memory
clocks in. Chill, Jake says, it was
just Syzygy, kid, the conjunction
of three heavenly bodies.

Angela Kirby

We were at the lake's edge, nothing for fifty miles.
September and the first freeze glinting between wet stones,
a death crackle in the still green leaves.
Sudden sun, we launched the canoe, headed west.

September and the first freeze glinting between wet stones.
You said the spirit took our June memory, turned it into today,
sudden sun. We launched the canoe, headed west,
boomeranging back to the first time we met.

You said the spirit took our June memory, turned it into today.
Your mouth teaching me those blunt Chipewyan vowels,
boomeranging back to the first time we met.
I try not to count the days.

Your mouth teaching me those blunt Chipewyan vowels,
us picking cranberries, no sugar to make jam.
I try not to count the days,
watch the wooden pier ice over.

Us picking cranberries, no sugar to make jam,
a death crackle in the still green leaves.
Watch the wooden pier ice over.
We were at the lake's edge, nothing for fifty miles.

Fiona Ritchie Walker

Nudibranch

were they floral
there would be songs for
sea-slugs too

Choisui 1813, translation by Robin D. Gill

If he could see me now: dribbling
like a sea-slug –

a shell-less regal goddess
dreaming of him

in naked, soft-bodied,
sea-going sleep.

If he could see me now
the way I sleep:

over-washed flannel pyjamas,
buttons missing,

old knickers, toxic breath –
the dribbling –

he wouldn't thank me
for these kisses we share:

jelly-body, rubbed by waves –
a sea-slug dreaming of him

at the bottom of my shallow
love-resistant bed.

Hilda Sheehan

A Wire to Grief

When you flash upon me,
yanking the voice from my throat,
I'm usually peeling potatoes
or combing my just-woken hair

or, worse, in bed with my not-quite-lover
who's helped pull me clear.
And you freeze me: peeler,
hairbrush, almost-lover in hand,

like that giant iguana I once saw
suddenly play dead, one foot high
in the air as if it was having a laugh,
not petrified, like me.

You rip all sound from the room
so it slips, cliffs rise, drop away.
There's that pause when nothing happens
before everything does; and I'm falling

like David Niven in *A Matter of Life and Death*
when his bombed Spitfire plunges, and he pleads
to be spared – he loves the radio control chick
on the line he's never even met.

Through the smoke and flames
I see, for a second, a reprieve for me, too –
if I had another life, I'd never walk out again,
leaving me and you just hanging.

Justina Hart

Virginity

Lost in a cramped flat, gas fire on,
Echo and the Bunnymen on low,

I want you back. Taken on the floor,
in five quick stabs, you're someone else's.

It was lonely in the bathroom without you,
where a week of bleeding started, splashed

on to school socks. A clothes horse straddled
the bath, his wife's bras, knickers dripped.

Gone in minutes, my yoke of fifteen years,
discovered at a disco, his fingers tugging

at you in the outside dark. Come back,
for a wedding, for the making of a life.
This time, leave me trembling, absolved.

Rebecca Goss

All My Thoughts

I didn't take your face between my hands
like a cup filled to the brim with water
or trace the outline of your shoulders
or learn the grace of each separate part.

I learnt nothing of your language,
but watched your glasses steam up
as you passed from street to pub
then slowly clear again, two ghosts

disintegrating on the lens. I didn't
walk the edges of the sea, or learn
how a border shifts like smoke,
only knew you, wrapped inside your coat.

We stood, my forehead pressed against
your chest, your hand stroking my hair.
I couldn't look at you or speak,
you whispered *tell me, tell me* and this

felt like a forgotten hurt, your lips
on mine, while the birds of my thoughts
wheeled overhead and the life (the life
I knew) called to me in sadness

open, let me in and so I did. I watched
you go and all the wolves and all
the stars went with you and I
walked back, back across the bridge.

Kim Moore

A Late Love Poem

I didn't think I'd feel like this
when I bumped into you on the Penrith line

after twenty-four years
three months and seven days.

I didn't think it would feel like a guard
demanding the fare I'd already paid.

Maggie Norton

I wrote *Don't worry. You're in hospital and I'll come and see you*
every day. You're ill and the doctors will make you better

and I suddenly thought of the seven brothers turned to swans
and how their sister, silent in her tower, spent years
weaving shirts from nettles to make them well.

And I wrote *I've labelled your wash-bag and your little radio*
and this is our phone number and I've got your wedding ring.
Don't worry. I wrote this in a brown notebook with a big JOHN
on the cover.

          I took you poetry because your memory
could hold a poem but nothing longer and you read only poems
in the first two months of this quite mild winter and I drove
every day on the long wet roads to visit you.

When I saw your ward and the men quiet in their beds
I thought of the swan enchantment – you were all mysteries
to the nurses and doctors weaving you nettle shirts.
Orphaned, retired, you said *Tell my parents and tell them at work*
and the man opposite suddenly dumb and the one at your side
paralysed and in pain for no reason. There was no diagnosis.

I said you were doing fine, having lots of tests and they'd soon
find out what was the matter. And I was fine, thank you.
But it wasn't soon and I wasn't fine and the only day I cried
I was like a burst main and I drove on the flooded roads
through the rain in a car full of tears. I saw
the great white foot of the turbine nudging the road,
the wind arms lost in rain and mist.

You were all swans, lost, far out over grey waters
creaking slowly along in the fog with no recollection of landfall.
But the shirts were finished after seven years except for a sleeve
and one of the brothers, though cured, had a swan's wing for an arm.

          Then you read me a poem
and I filled in your menu card and fed you tangerines
and you said how you liked the nurses, they were so kind.
When I went you determined to see me to the door.
Then I had to see you back to your own ward –
you were vague about which one it was –
and you wanted politely to see me out again.

Stay here, I said *They're going to make you well.*

Carole Coates

Deep Forest

for Christophe

When you said 'Are we going into the unknown?
I'm very familiar with it', I laughed.
We laughed together but I wrote your words

on a small piece of paper
and they merged with something I had just read
about coming

> *to the borders of sleep,*
> *The unfathomable deep*
> *Forest where all must lose*
> *Their way ...*

I wonder how you can live so intimate with the unknown,
so close it becomes like your tweed jacket and peaked cap, your small cigar,
which will all become strange, unworded, one day,

or like your family, your familiars: who are those
backs of men sitting at my table, who don't speak to me,
don't seem to know me, make me invisible in my own house?

Things become half-worded, like the packet of camel mile:
'Difficult to fit in a cupboard, a mile of camels',
you joke, and mean the puzzlement too.

I know it in glimpses – a black and white jacket,
but the face drops away, or a scent lingers beside me but
a name has gone. The deep forest brushes past, comes nearer –

close as the stranger in the hospital bed beside mine
whose daughters stood around her all night
like dark waiting trees.

Sue MacIntyre

The lines in italics are from Edward Thomas's 'Lights Out'

Mal Culottée

Le bon Roi Dagobert
avait mis sa culotte à l'envers.
Le grand Saint Eloi lui dit:
'O mon roi,
Votre Majesté est mal culottée'.
'Eh bien,' lui dit le roi,
'Je vais la remettre à l'endroit'.

Old Nursery Rhyme

We call it 'hoisting the sails', when she's at half-
mast or has the 'sails' flapping round her ankles
as I come in from work to find her laughing
or arguing in French with long-lost uncles.

She smiles: ' I often talk to myself, did
you know?' – face glowing with animation.
'Did *you* know that your knickers aren't even mid-
way up?' She chuckles, shrugs away convention.

But she's uncomfortable and sore and soaking
and as I soap and talc her clean and dry –
ad-libbing forgotten bits of *We are Sailing* –

'The things I ask you to do for me,' she sighs.
I hoist the sails. 'But nothing you didn't do
for me', I say. She nods, 'That's very true'.

Lucy Hamilton

By Heart

Once she had to memorize the chemical elements
of soil, learn how to measure the height of trees
using sine and cosine and how to address a letter
to a bishop – information lost now in dusty
box files in a corner of her brain, with lists
of Latin verbs and conjugations, the Attributes
of the Virgin Mary and which feast days a priest
wore rose or purple. But she remembers maples
graded from cinnabar to porphyry stretching
across the Laurentian hills like reels of Sylko
in a haberdasher's drawer; the rustle of raven wings
through cedars as an Indian canoe skims the surface
of a turquoise lake; castles carved from blocks
of ice, snow on the windshield as she left.

Margaret Beston

Barefoot in the Snow

It's Africa, a safari, a trek
in heat, flies and more heat.
Lion calls drown the air
as the tall barefoot man guides
us to the waterhole.
Our packs, heavy, we struggle,
stumble into the murky wallow
of mud and elephant dung to coolness.

Unlike the coldness of grandmother's
bared feet as she trekked, distressed,
into that Norwegian winter night,
arctic moon over deep snow,
following her lost guide,
lost to his own self, lost
to his home and hearth,
circling straight northwards
towards his childhood.

Feet beyond thawing, she led
him back to his unfamiliar bed.

Diana Moen Pritchard

Room of the Three Windows

I read the facts out loud as if they're poems:
Machu Picchu's hitching post of the sun,
its room of the three windows, how, on certain dates,
the pillar cast no shadow at all.

Too weak now to open the lid of his laptop,
he asks me to find his other photographs –
Giza, Tikal, Stonehenge – talks of 'anti-gravity',
as if this explains their miracles of weightlessness,

how solid tons of rock could float up mountains
to become chairs and kneeling pads of gods.
He's staring out of the hospital window
wondering how ever he lifted the stones

of marriage, fatherhood, career. Later,
he's the first to see the snow arrive,
grateful for the way it lets him lose
the measure of this unbelieving world.

All evening he drifts into its slow whiteness
till midnight brings him to a high place
where he finds no shadows. Anti-gravity: he has mastered
the art. Nurses note the date, hour, approximate minute.

Rosie Jackson

Knight Move

How we could all come to love the road,
to want to be travellers, driving the highway,
the sun behind us, following the truck
with the soldiers singing.
If I could play that game of chess again
you'd win because I'd be too slow to make
a move. The sun on its chosen path would pursue
your words, *this is the last time we'll laugh like this.*
                        To be on a road that led
from nowhere to here, turn right at crossroads
into early sunrises, bright kitchens, the cream frozen
on the doorstep milk; if I could do all this I'd learn
how to take your bishop, change your move.
You'd have been the one to join in with whoever was singing.

Wendy French

Honshū bees

When my father went to bed, and stayed there
the bees arrived
to do all the things he could not do.

With their jointed legs they lifted
shreds of tobacco from his pouch
and turned round and round in the bowls of his pipes
till carbon clung to their fur.

They burnished his fountain pen, wafted open his diary
playing back to themselves his separate hours
settling on the fine lines between days.

Each bee bent its head and focused its triple eyes
on the shut wings of the *f*s and the *g*s
until another language rose into view
compacted of honey and memory.

And with that knowledge they flew upstairs
to where he slept his deep gold sleep
and walked into his head, one by one
carrying his syllables back to him, after fifty years.

Dorothy Yamamoto

Five things I saw before my mother died

'mon cuer entier' my whole heart –
from a medieval love ring

with clarity the brimstone
crosses the garden
light through yellow

light without forethought
'mon cuer entier' on its
sleeve   the half leaf

I'd look through
for purity
before the rose

heavies the air before
honeysuckle drifts
through the east window

   *

whichever is first
loss   longing
the erosion of choice

your heart will stop
and be silent
he'll make you a garden   for

something
to do with
his hands

   *

I find myself
in so many ways
thinking about you

translating   as if we spoke
several languages
none of them well

   *

under the netting
that guards
the soft fruit

imprecise words
gleam through the foliage
we pick them too late

bletted
in the mouth
and red as blood

*

let's take a phrase
and listen
it's so hard

to hear
the message
light is easier

it might fall
across you
just so

you might
wear
it

Janet Sutherland

Gardening With Deer

And now you know for yourself how it is.
The ragged hours' breathing,
long nights and longer days.
Watching her shift in her sleep,
as the moon turns and skies alter
and the ghost-trees of early morning
are heavy with frosted leaves
like a fruit of hanging doves.

A lifetime of gardening with deer,
their rough noses huffing
over the fence, nipping at the roses.
Fraying the bark of saplings
to remove the velvet, their heads
laid against the trunks. The stag
whipping the branches with his antlers.

All this is remembered in a still room
where the spirit of the white deer
with an arrow in his heart
walks through her dreamtime,
and the sweet musky sigh of roebuck
in the back of her throat
rises with every breath.
You hold her hand,
anxious, yet dreading her waking.

Kathy Miles

Dyeing the Corpse's Hair

There is no smell of death in the funeral parlor
when my daughter arrives to help prepare
her mother-in-law for the casket. Nothing
is shocking here. She looks almost herself

yet completely other. It had been sudden,
that unnoticed wasting, it had shrivelled her.
Her arms lie lax, lacking the bones she'd willed
for marrow-harvest, though her swollen heart's

unusable any more. Her neglected hair has taken
the embalming fluid up unevenly
in bright pink patches, a flower set
in a vase of ink. How she would hate

to arrive in heaven looking worse
than she would look going to Mass, to the store,
and so my daughter dyes her hair for her
there in the funeral parlor basement.

Light Ash, the color she always used.
Tinted water runs off through the channels
to the bucket beneath the table, as other fluids.
Her skin is cold, but dry, not clammy,

and pressure dents it like raw pastry,
earrings must be placed right first time.
My daughter paints her nails for her, makes up
her face under the mortician's instructions

because no one but family must do this.
There's a special foundation to go on first,
beneath the Rimmel, and this too must be right
first time. My daughter's good at makeup.

Lastly they dress her in the new dress
three sizes smaller,
chosen for her by her granddaughters
when the youngest asked *Is she dead for ever?*

My daughter calls me to tell me everything,
we're crying across the Atlantic down the phone,
and in spite of myself
I'm noting everything down.

Joanna Boulter

The radio clock

The accuracy is praiseworthy, we said,
contemplating the loss or gain
of one second in every million years.

The radio clock on our bedroom mantelpiece
believed in time: one second
followed another like a confident decision.

It thought time would last
for ever. We too
were fond of time, the flow of time,

its arrow pointing
to the future. We held
the future like presents

we couldn't yet open;
there were stars and trees, silver
and blue and gold, on the paper.

We did not think
about lost presents, or a time
when presents stopped.

Outside the snow fell...
it did not melt.
We had the exuberance of snow.

*

So emphatic a conjunction. The dent
of our bodies on the bed

as they merged like minute merging into minute
became their dent in the fabric of space-time.

We were comfortable living in time; the melting
of snow did not yet threaten us.

Our landscape was snow, shining and crisp;
holding our days it seemed to sweep

into the distance.

*

I said *Is there a way to predict avalanches?* –
that helter skelter of minutes rushing
towards destruction, shifting the soft snow,

as when the hands of the radio clock raced round
to catch up with a new time. The clock
had no answers, knew nothing

of the loss of days.

Daphne Gloag

Vision

I was leaving London, leaving England,
standing the North Atlantic between death
and absence when my taxi jolted to a stop.
A gust had snatched the glasses from a man
about as old as you, hair turning grey,
and dropped them in the road. As I watched,
the car in front of us drove over the fragile
plastic. You were safe, two weeks buried,
and the blinded man, unharmed, yet I felt
my body inside your body fall and shatter
as if we were his glasses. The frames were wrecked.
He tried but could not pick up all the pieces.

Joan Michelson

Night

You turn to marble
a Rodin or a Canova
against the pillow

your breath noiseless
as the moonlight at our window
silent as my handkerchief

a wasteful silence
upholstered by grief
windows shrouded with net

one small spider weaves a web
in the corner of the room
veils my face against the world.

Jean Hall

Red Sarong

for Diane

My thinking
not thus
(Sappho Fragment 3)

The delivery man arrives with a bouquet
of well-wishers' thoughts. You kiss him. (What else
on a hot summer day when all is not well?)
You gather loose leaves of Thai silk
into your hands, those flow-freeing folds
red and black and wringing with sweat
from that sultry day as you walk into the house
to replenish the jug with fresh lemon and water.
It's the characteristic hold of your skirt
that confuses for this moment life and death
(who we should kiss)
and just when we are desperately clinging to skirts
someone catches a memory.

Wendy French

Everlasting Expanding Rings 1

I found in August, after he died,
hidden in a snowy-flowered bush
a dunnock's nest. Its open cup,
bound fast to twigs, and neatly made
of roots and moss, was lined with silver hair.
This was so smoothly-laid and silky-soft
it could have been newclipped
and dropped that day onto the sunwarmed flags
outside the kitchen door. He hated barbers;
and so he sat there on a stickbacked chair,
a towel round his shoulders, and I snipped –
inexpertly – the fine thinning hair,
once thick and brown, and dropped it there
in summer after summer. More than comfort,
it gives almost unseemly joy
to see those wisps recycled in a cradle.

Anna Adams

Birdsong in Budapest

A bird wakes me and I hurry to the window
like being summoned, and in the one tree, so close
it almost touches the glass – the bird,

dove-grey in early light, its little mouth
turning the air with a five-boned tongue,
into a song. And as it sings, along the street

to right and left, the windows gleam and quiver,
and the roofs of the parked cars reflect
its shivery brilliance. Under my feet

the parquet vibrates, and the whole house
moves as the nameless bird returns to earth
what keeps getting lost, a particular thing

to belong to, the song, very old and invisible,
which brings to mind every morning, a reminder
of something small but expressible, I want to find.

Gill Horitz

A Life

for Joan

How ripples of clay
move up the pot
like breath –

How a newborn
is a soul set in flesh,
given outward form –

How this suddenly shattered
human being
is like a broken pot –

Elizabeth Burns

Task

Here's your rain,
that specializes in you

Here's your fret of looking, your silvery silvern,
your year of song, worldly with light

Here's your heart, and all that it can do
What can it do?

Here's your *ange bon temps,*
your *ange mauvais*

Here's your thought,
clouds over mountains
honouring someone

Here's your summer, slowly passing

Here's your mouth, and all that it can do
What can it do?

Here's your fear,
its restive stubborn clockwork

Here's your dream, ex libris

Here's your hand, and all that it can do
What can it do?

Here's your lovely wilding
tall and shrewd and now in bloom

Here's your Mercredi,
your Vendredi,

your house, its ups and downs,
your sky, de dia, de noche,
your world and all that it can do

What can it do?

Penelope Shuttle

Section 4: ENQUIRING MINDS
thoughts, creativity, vision

And The Soul

> And the soul, if she is to know herself,
> must look inside the soul
>   Plato

And the soul, if she is to know herself
must look into the soul and find
what kind of beast is hiding.

And if it be a horse, open up the gate
and let it run. And if it be a rabbit
give it sand dunes to disappear in.

And if it be a swan, create a mirror image,
give it water. And if it be a badger
grow a sloping woodland in your heart.

And if it be a tick, let the blood flow
until it's sated. And if it be a fish
there must be a river and a mountain.

And if it be a cat, find some people
to ignore, but if it be a wolf,
you'll know from its restless way

of moving, if it be a wolf,
throw back your head
and let it howl.

Kim Moore

from *The Art of Falling*, Seren Books, 2015

What it Was

It was the pool and the blue umbrellas,
blue awning. It was the blue and white

lifesize chess set on the terrace, wall of jasmine.
It was the persimmon and palm side by side

like two wise prophets and the view that dipped
then rose, the swallows that turned the valley.

It was the machinery of the old olive press,
the silences and the voices in them calling.

It was the water talking. It was the woman
reading with her head propped, wearing glasses,

the logpile under the overhanging staircase,
mist and the mountains we took for granted.

It was the blue humped hose and living wasps
swimming on the surface. It was the chimneys.

It was sleep. It was not having a mother,
neither father nor mother to comfort me.

Mimi Khalvati

Jet Lag

I didn't go round the world. It went around me
crossing time zones in my sealed-off balloon,

following inflight-arrows across Europe,
Asia, Australia. Don't ask what day it is –

my body clock ticks in those concertinaed
intervals between borders and continents,

oceans urging them forward.
I can't find sleep. Instead I have birds

crisscrossing the lanes of my head.
They saw my airship slip by and me peering

through a window, setting my watch
by the stars. I'll catch up with this shaky life,

wrap it around me like a quick nap.
Leonardo put such problems on hold

with his *ornithopter,* needing wings
to flap before it could move.

So much for all that sky-gazing,
wanting to get off the ground.

Now I'll just sleep on possibilities.
I'm still thirty thousand feet up,

nudging clouds like a sunset, the day
slipping through my fingers.

Katherine Gallagher

Hanging

Like a raindrop suspended from a twig,
or the flower on the brink

of saying goodbye to its stalk,
history is hanging,

Along with the tyrant
and the woman who murdered her lover.

The countries adhere to the globe – just.

And the day is ratcheted
along all the stages of a crisis.

A day is not a compact thing.
Necks are bullish and vulnerable.

The boulders and the dust-motes.
Hang them.

The sun blinks and blinks
with grit in its eye.

As a child, I picked up my pen
and marvelled

how the ink clung in the nib,
the tiny miracle.

Moniza Alvi

Hermetic

1 Healing

> *Sepia,* said the homeopath.
> *What you need is sepia.*

Cuttlefish seep ink in ropy clouds.
Gratefully, the brain
relaxes into its own sea-medium; murky salts.
Dendrites drift and drink, drift and drink. Stuff of miracles.
A lemon-tree half-glimpsed behind
a city gate sends its axon
deep into the sepia strata which cover
the face of the earth.

And God said, *Let there be lemons. Let*
knobs of gold hang all over the heavens. Let there be
suns beyond telling.

Light flooded the yellow kitchen.
In his cage the canary awoke and hopped off
his perch for the sheer pleasure of swinging back on again;
then honed his beak, puffed out
his tiny throat feathers and addressed himself
to the business of day: singing.

Light danced on a bleached bone.

2 Space

> *After a painting by Victor Brauner*

In the beginning there were jars
and jars, and a canary singing. *Hermetically sealed,*
said Grandma; her slippers sprouted little wings as
she rested from her labours. Light
slanted through the apricots, cherries, plums,
and was transformed. The evening sun
trilled notes dyed pomegranate.
Alchemy. The knotted hands
wrought, and look.

From the palette seep tilted planes. Legs
and lips, eye-breast and arrow-heart dance in
a delicacy of desire. Male and Female
paints he them; see we them.
The oils glow. Forgotten the *Hermetica.*

Thief, herald . . . Even Hermes
might not simply take and give.
Necessity charged him: string
the tortoise-shell, distil the music.

This is the matter. How each space leaks
and spills, stains and weeps into its own alembic.
How the summer light nuzzles a peach from
out its leaf and touches its fuzz with gold.

Margaret Wilmot

Grey Matter

Look at this flint. Look at it –
grey, rounded, unbroken;
so unpretentious
as it simpers in my hand.
It wants you to like it,
it wants you to take its side,
to let it be, or, if you must,
at least split it cleanly.

But watch – all the time
its tightly-fitted skin
is only just managing
to hold in its secrets.
The lives of past creatures,
their form and formation,
contained, and stored,
in a petrified jelly core.

Don't be fooled. Here –
put your hand upon it.
Be as stern as you like,
for you are its master.
Demand that it falls apart
of its own accord.
In that moment, for you,
new thinking will be born.

Victoria Pugh

Trilobite

Remember, as a child, how someone would shout *Catch!*
and too old to refuse, and too young not to,
the body's coordinates not quite set

this object, moving in an arc towards you
somehow created you, trembling, outstretched?
That's how it came to me, this trilobite,

a present from the underworld, a stern familiar
hopelessly far-fetched. What it wanted from me
I never knew, its hard parts being its only parts,

the three parts of its crossways nature
cephalos, thorax, pigidium
as later, now, I've learned to call them,

carrying a memory of itself like water
as my fingers moved on its captive body,
the feathery stone of its cool guitar.

It reminded me of a woodlouse, too,
the honesty of small, friendly things.
But the metallic gleam of its smoothed edges

were taut and innocent as an unfired gun.
So it bedded in, leaving behind a gleaming trail
as a biro bleeding in a pocket might,

a puff of ink from a hounded squid.
And my skin shimmered
with its silvery threads, and my breath quickened

as it wrote my body, left a garden of knowing in damp tattoos.
The further I threw it, the closer it came.
Sometimes, alone, I'd ask it questions

stroke it like a secret pet.
How deep is the ocean? What's the blueness of blue?
How is the earth as you lie inside it?

It would reply in a voice both
high-pitched and enduring, or
whisper like a ghost till only silence remained.

And left me only when I'd learned to love it,

small as a bullethole,
in the place where it pressed itself,
its fossil colours close to my heart.

Last night, unable to sleep,
it nudged its way back into my life,
pulling me from the fragrant pillow

to perch once again on my naked shoulders,
to drop like a coin in my offered hand.
Beside me, my husband slept.

And the fact of its presence, its subtle truth,
was something to touch,
like the wounds of Christ;

its transformation as I went to kiss it,
a wafer on the pushed-out tongue.

Deryn Rees-Jones

A Perfect Rain

> 'the lit bush' from *The Bright Field*
> R S Thomas

Imagine the past. Isn't that what we do?
Lay down trace after trace of cobweb remembering.
Even the rip that runs transverse
to all we think is written in our blood only exists
because we dream it does.
The perfect rain falls down
and building is what creatures,
do, a smear of clay,
a past,
a patiently fitted twig.
Few can praise
the lit bush
for what it is,
simply transfigured by a morning.

Kate Foley

The gift

Once you were given an unwrapped box.
There was no paper to tear, no velvet ribbon coiling
to the floor, only a bone-white lid to lift.

Inside was darkness – an empty night that made
your head spin, echoed with the thud of your heart.
You hid the box away on a high shelf

filled the air with light, radio static,
the chatter of television. But a shadow
seeped from under the lid, a whisper of anxiety

muffling all sound with the smell of winter –
shades of tobacco, charcoal, ink.
So you took the box down again

allowed its silence to flow over bookcase, sofa
the one cup on the table, to marble the walls
like the reflection of sunlit water.

Yvonne Baker

Birthday Owl

for J.

When you brought it to me
wrapped in blue paper, tied with tinselly ribbon,

I opened it gingerly, surprised at your miniature gift:
faceted crystal, one inch tall,

set on a tiny plinth – unblinking topaz eyes
a shining creature, conduit for light.

You picked it up, *t'-whit-t'-whoo-ed*,
gliding around the room, the night forest close

with eerie calls, a witch's moon, and you
a six-year-old in love with this

glass-feathered bird on its
unbreakable perch –

our barn owl swooping –
in, out – in

and out – daring the sky...

Katherine Gallagher

A Chinese Lacquer Egg

Something is beginning. We feel it in the raw edges
of our dreams, our bodies hostage to light, to weather.
It is filling us with the weight of summer
which floats like helium through our wintered bones.
We wonder at it all, surprised by warmth, a sudden downpour,
the ruffled line of birdsong, a forgotten bulb
forcing its way through sodden earth towards the sun.
Or this Chinese lacquer egg, which appeared one morning
in my outstretched palm. Beyond the sound
of aeroplane or train, as we drift asleep, hands cupped
to the pillow, it shares its oval mysteries. Listen!
Between breath and silence it is showing itself.
In these shortened nights it is not unlike rapture,
an unworded prayer its indelible hum.

Deryn Rees-Jones

Ignominy

Withal I know the lovely lone laboriousness of being

like cloud in the making.

I stand, alone, mistaken

in undress.

The crows erupt, like words, around me –

Lord, Lord –

with all their raucousness.

Gillian Allnutt

from *after Kandinsky*

8 Tension in Red – (1926)

Every secret is a hidden box. You rein it in
and wait. Years on, you've stored laughter
to keep you steady. The sky flares red,
its fires savage the forest.
      You remember
when the arsonists cried *wolf*
and their calls defeated you.

As the sun climbs, the sky is strummed
like a guitar – string-ladders of sound.
You see the dispute between red and black,
light offered to travellers between moons.

Red stretches, soars, spills,
      tantalizes ...

Katherine Gallagher

Notes on a Bonfire

I did it in one match. The sheep moved but were not alarmed.
      Good northwesterly.
Contortion of twigs giving themselves to fire; explosions, mostly
      small.

Stems ready and not ready to burn; some lengths remaining sullen,
      some glorying.
Leaves of prunings twizzling up. At times the wind swings and
      flames claw out.

(Why are we offended by inconsistency?) (Old lion in the shabby
      zoo, snoozing,
only the wire between us. I jumped before I knew he had thrown
      his fire-look.)

Sky a thin equinoctial blue, grass yellow-green. Tongues of pouring
      smoke.
Shadow of smoke on the green more solid than the smoke itself
      against blue.

Red heat crawls up a branch, pauses, writhes, and flame shakes out
                                                  like a dragon-
fly from the casing of a nymph. (Would you say that the nymph is
                                                  dead?)

Dragonfly becomes hair, seaweed, rag, feather, thong. Tending and
                                                  feeding
and raking; wanting more. (If you provoke me too much I may
                                                  lionmouth you.)

Later the fire's withdrawn but still formidable. Later still, flagging:
                                                  dying,
it seems, but the skin of my forehead's as tight as parchment in the
                                                  heat.

Sun's gone down. All I've dragged there, a red eye in the field. Soft,
                                                  soft,
tomorrow's ash. (But a child ran across a firebed like that, scorched
                                                  her bare soles for days.)

I want to revive this fire, burn up rake, shed, house, trees, me. And I
                                                  don't
want to revive it. I'm in love with transformation and it frightens
                                                  me.

Bone-fire: scar and char. It's raining and I'm going in. I see that I
                                                  don't

want to be cremated, I'm a slow mover. I must change my will.

M R Peacocke

The Self Portrait

I thought to draw my living mask,
    with lines, or light and dark,
so propped a glass up on my desk
    and made a charcoal mark.

But in the ground below my room –
    deep in the shadow-well –
a narrow desert longed to bloom
    and so I left my cell

and softly, down the spiral stair,
    crept to a bolted door
and, stepping out into the air,
    proceeded to explore.

Laurels intensified the shade;
    I pruned and thinned, then found
green ferns, and planted more, I made
    small areas of ground

by prising up the trodden stones
    and digging deep; I fed
manure, dried blood and crumbled bones
    into the barren bed

then sought out flowers to make bright
    the semidarkness; most
were toxic as the aconite
    or pallid as a ghost,

but all took root and grew. Pale fire
    shone in the gloom; bile-green
proliferated; nightshade bore
    black phials of atropine.

The belladonna that arrests
    man's heart, grew tall and thrived,
and henbane, on forbidden lists
    of killers, I reprieved.

When I had climbed the secret stair
    and sat again, and drew,
my smiling likeness hinted where
    the true self-portrait grew.

Anna Adams

The mathematician

From his window, he could see snow falling as the fractals
he couldn't see but which he relied on being there.

There were numbers lost at the end of his imagination
like countries so far away he'd never make it to them.

A shadow fell and then he heard a crack as of glass:
below, against the conservatory, an icicle

like an organ pipe or stalactite of diamond
had shattered into its pieces of supercooled clarity.

He thought of her skin: it was as seductive of light
as ice. It was impossible to talk to her.

On a sheet of paper, he began a series of equations:
numbers teaming up as water does, irresistible to itself

in the cold, numbers aligning like the tracks of a sledge
in unmeeting parallel. Then they writhed like meltwater.

He held a set of keys for locks that may not exist.
Or was he shadowing the word that set the world ringing?

The dusk was growing deeper. Houses on the other side
of the horizon began switching on their lights

and he also reached for his lamp. There were some things
of which he could be certain. The rest was love.

Jemma Borg

Funambulist

Ambulatory on the silver blade,
solitude helps me
concentrate my muscles and thoughts,
check my centre of gravity.

I wear satin shoes with leather soles
and feel sharpness beneath them.
Trying not to press down
on the knife-edge I move as soon as I can

to the next step, wanting to know more.
I skip, point my toe,
lower then raise myself, balance
with one leg lifted in front, arabesque.

This is what I do.
In other places I may have lived
a different sort of life.
Have I been made to do this?

Some say there is a finishing point
but it stretches away
and I cannot see the end. It doesn't mean
there isn't one. Some speak of a wall.

Tension is my territory; unreleasing.
Light falling in patterns
beneath me where it shines,
sand grains glistering.

There is ascent and descent.
To the left and right, desert
and knife-edge dunes,
sand ships with their indigo sails.

Pat Marum

Royal Engineer's Wife, 1944

Midnight and he's in there again, bent over
his notebook, scribbling computations,
working his slide rule as if exorcising a demon.

He won't talk to me, just mutters to himself
about tides, anchors, shear. *For the war effort,*
is all he'll say, but he's possessed by this problem.

His brow furrowed as farm fields, cuticles bitten
to bleeding. Of course he's tired. We're all weary,
trying to keep calm and carry on.

But this is different. Something is afoot. Something
big, risky, lurking on the murky edges of possibility.
I shuffle to the kitchen, make him another cup of tea.

Tomorrow I shall go without. For the war effort.

Kathleen M Quinlan

Boatbuilder

From a walnut face his eyes
mirror the sky like moorland tarns.
He carries a toolbag
with hammers, adze, brace and bit,
saws, spokeshave, nails and clamps.

By the river we are building a boat:
plank by plank our hull takes shape
and hammers sound its drum. Buzz
of saw pauses when rotten wood clunks
to the pile. We drink pine-scented air.

Gaps are caulked with oakum and tar,
our mast is hauled and slotted, bolt upright.
As she slips into the water I hold my breath
but she floats; wind catches the sails
he has set, carrying our craft away.

Jean Watkins

Path

She prepared the ground to take him to and from the door.
Their home backed due north into the rising moor.
He had know-how, skill, an ailing body;
so, from the threshold, he guided her to lay
four thousand bricks upon ten tons of sand.

Her hands roughskinned with grit she laid drainage,
boundaries unsecured by granite were made sound.
She encouraged the hill to fall kind to the eye, then
barrowed in four thousand bricks, ten tons of sand.

Down the falling camber of the hill
the herringbone of brick to brick came slow.
Edges required angle grinder, mask, chisel,
until, in fading light, a few score bricks in hand,
she strewed, dusted in, the last remains of sand.

Hilary Jupp

Felt

She stranded the oily fleece
washed, not spun,
then trod it between cloths.
A small piece, to show me.

The dye she chose was blood.
She made me copy every step,
looking into my face
to make sure I knew.

I remember bony fingers
smoothing the wool,
a baby crying somewhere till
the stream's clatter soothed it.

With it my childhood fell away
trodden, then squeezed into a round
under my hands. What could I make from this?
Slippers, a cap, a child's toy.

Sue Aldred

Catch and Release

In my mind I see her
take a strand of silk
a feather
a tuft of hair gleaned from the dog
dreaming on the rug

she makes a tiny insect
adds a hook like a strange curved limb
tapering to a point

I see her go through the heather
to where the river pours like glass
over granite
and specks of sunlight roam the quiet pools

she stands thigh deep
rod arching, line
flickering like the tongue of a snake

the fly lands, kisses the water
teasing, testing
flicks up, settles again upstream

she feels the tug, eases the line
lets it run, reels in, drawing them together
easing and pulling till the game is won

she lifts the fish, takes out the hook
slips it in the stream again
a flash of silver and it's gone.

Back in the world of books
she leans on the lectern, pencil poised
ties wisps of thought
into a question
lands it lightly among us
and we take it, run with it
while she concedes, then slowly draws us in
until the argument is won
she slips us free.

Jenna Plewes

Bird

Installation by Anselm Kiefer

Even if you hate installations
there's an element of purity
about this mammoth recycling of books
                              as bird
        its wings   tatty notebooks
the pages torn or falling out
their whiff of damp or char
        like scorched feathers

        reminding me of the fire sales
she took me to as a child
   my sewing grandma   the one
who made things

        There were shelves and tables
covered with tall bolts of cloth their edges
hideously singed   her hands reverent
as she unrolled each unpromising bundle
planning curtains   planning
voluminous skirts
        chintz-covered cushions
                        rose covered coats
   their blossoms
bursting to escape
        and in her eyes
the pride of the scavenger

        Think road-kill   red-tailed kites
their wing-span a fraction
the size of this ragged specimen
   but functional   earning their right
to the sky   the planet

Wendy Klein

Raku

The golden bowl has faded
  to a dull sea-green.
    Its blackened foot-ring

still smells of the burning
  sawdust which smothered its all
    but molten body, starving it

of air till it fed off its own
  oxygen. Long gone the moment
    of blazing, the golden bowl held

in tongs at arms' length, tipped free
  of acrid sawdust, cooled in water,
    set on a brick to dry.

Judith Cair

White

Almost the last thing he made in this life
was the collage in white:
a still-life abstracted to texture

and shape, gradations of shade
as if it had gathered into itself
all the colour-soaked world;

everything he had absorbed
pared down to a whiteness
like that of the masses of narcissi

all swaying in the wind
or the wings of the whooper swans
rising over the estuary

or this bowl made of porcelain,
its rim so fine
the white becomes translucent.

Elizabeth Burns

Owl

When my heart stopped, I fell from the tree.
He picked me out of the mud,
stroked my head, wiped my beak on his shirt.

In the room, he sets me on a white plinth,
lays out worms of colour to give me back my life,
ochre, burnt umber, vermillion.

He bathes me in a pale wash on a white page,
releases my limbs with his soft strokes,
the tips of my primaries flash like arrows.

He opens my midnight eyes. Then waters run together,
my wings flow out. He sucks his lips, sponges the wet,
I drift into tawny furrows, mingle with woodland.

In a dry mood, he rakes lines with a fork
along my feathery back: I am a strip of bark
on my favourite oak, I disappear, he can't find me.

He is dwindling now, pale and small as the beak
he once wiped with the sleeve of his shirt.
I fly low, listening for long grass tickle-sounds.

Jill Eulalie Dawson

The Lost Library of Jesi

They handled them with cotton gloves. Leather covers
tooled in gold, paper from Fabriano, printed woodcuts

from Bologna: manuscripts, almanacs, books of poetry
and philosophy, science and history; mappa mundi

and the first edition of the Divine Comedy. They lifted
bookshelves, levered panels from the walls

and as they worked the sun spilled centuries of light
through slits in the shutters across the marble tiles

until behind the coffered panels they found fissured stones
opening to a sealed room windowless and cool

with fallen columns below a hemispheric dome
and shadows curled asleep in empty niches along the walls.

They crawled inside that chamber's deepest quiet
where one or two could still hear the beating of a heart.

Caroline Maldonado

All These Heavy Books

pressed in their shelves
like rigid butterflies on pins.

You hear the fustiness
which crusts each page
like dust that once exploded
in a city blitz, their patina
no more than *déjà vu.*

And yet you cleave to them
like leaves on winter twigs,
believe they hold the sum
of all you've been.

Are they god-like volumes
preaching with double tongues?
Tomb-stones you would have
around as touch-stones?

Or do they whisper through
the rustle of page after page,
Get rid of us, for where you go
words hold no weight? By then
you'll know the buoyancy of space.

Gill Nicholson

Somewhere

in the lining
of her head
a sepia photo, unframed,
of what her poem could be about.

In the study cobwebs
trespass over Virago books
high shelves where baby spider
plants suspend in air
her mind is sifting spaces
sewing gossamer thread
through nooks and crannies
amongst rows of women's books.

Now intent on fetching scissors
snipping ties and spinning
this imaginary yarn
of enchanted craft
she will lift her head
brush back a strand of hair
and follow spiders with that pencil,
trailing desolate landscapes
over fifty sheets of unlined paper.

Somewhere
in Devon
a run-down cottage, framed
in an old oak doorway
Father stands, his cheeks amazed
by frost,
proudly bearing in armfuls –
of the last of his spring cabbage.

Julie Sampson

Scaling the Herrings

She lays down her pen. It is finished now, she thinks. Through
the open window she can see the long folds of the downs,
catch the scent of wistaria and lilac.

He wanders in. Have you seen my keys? I thought I'd left them
in the hall. She shakes her head. Isn't the wistaria wonderful?
Look, what do you think of this? Is it finished? Does it work?

He is rummaging though the papers on her desk, strews them
over the floor. Where are those damned keys? God, I hate the smell
of wistaria. I'm starving, when will lunch be ready?

Soon, she says, piles her papers back on the desk, puts the poem
in her pocket and goes into the kitchen; it smells of dog and fish.
She picks up a thin knife, begins to scale and slit the herrings.

Using her thumb, she pushes out the guts, wipes bloody fingers
on her apron, with the edge of her palm presses the spines,
lifts out fans of bones, smears mustard on the flesh.

A staccato of angry typing from the study; he's having trouble
with his last chapter; everything she does today will be wrong.
She dusts the herrings with oatmeal, fries them in smoking oil.

I'm going out, he shouts, the front door slams. She throws away
the fish, treats herself to tea and raspberry jam, thinks of Gumilev
snarling to Akhmatova, Get into the kitchen, clean the herrings.

The lilac in the white jug droops, wistaria drifts by the window,
a blackbird trebles to his mate. She sighs, fingers the poem
in her pocket, thinks How wonderful to be a blackbird.

Angela Kirby

Moorish Home

for Mimi Khalvati

In our hanging house, one wall sheer to the dry riverbank,
rooms staggering across split levels, the hours are sticky

with fever and all I see of you is a passing shadow climbing
the stairs opposite my open door. We spend our days apart

but in the evenings we walk and distribute our greetings, *Hola,
Buenos Noches*, to the people in the street, or exchange

Farsi for Hebrew: *Laila Tov*, we say to each other, *Shabékheyr*.
Last night we talked of Córdoba, alliance of Muslim and Jew,

and you pulled me back for a moment – *this is how it was, this!* –
when we strolled past a woman cooking barbeque on the steps

of the village square, a man (*her* man?) humming a cante jondo
to his father. You were wearing my gipsy shawl and I,

slipping back to the Golden Age, began to compose a gacela
as Lorca called them. How easily it built in my sleep, couplets

folding into themselves like accordion scales, rising from kitchen
to living room to the vine shaded terrace where you lay

on the rattan chair, smoking, always smoking, and in my sleep
we became Al-Ghazali and Halevi, dreaming of *this*: a new Jerusalem.

Aviva Dautch

Notes: *Buenos Noches* (Spanish), *Laila Tov* (Hebrew) and *Shabékheyr*
(Farsi) all mean 'Good Night'. The medieval Spanish Jewish poet Judah
Halevi was greatly influenced by Persian Sufi philosopher Al-Ghazali.
Ghazali's name translates as 'The Ghazal Writer', Halevi's as 'The Priest'.

Word Clouds

Words in the cloud
tagged like lost balloons.
A whiffle of starlings in a quiet dawn
skimming the lip of sky.
Recycled sentences and phrases
crowding the atmosphere.

Whilst earth, humming sweetly to itself
– a thrum of low notes –
shucks off cars, houses, people,
cracks roads apart, a wet dog
shaking his head to cause tsunami.

And there is the shift-shape of cells
swelling, ebbing. The sudden unfamiliar:
air-change, break of ice,
currents swifting the wrong way
the alchemy of melting glaciers.

As polar caps thaw, seal-pods wane,
language diminishes, a shrinking river
of text. And as the white bear
seeks an ice-flow, so words search
for home in the entropy of the tongue.

But the birds' song shrills
in the air, migrates across
a shrivel of continents.
Storks nestle onto chimney stacks,
starlings roost in remembered places.

When the birds stop coming
we will know the time is here
the final murmuration
that we will see, or hear.

Kathy Miles

Song

She did for me with the first pluck
on her strung gourd spilling outward
like rings of water and the long wail
leading into her song of Krishna
and kingfishers, of how to ride
the crest of the wave without drowning.
She was all toothless gums
stained with paan juice, her throat a cave.
People said, when she needed firewood
she made the tree in her yard drop a branch.
I shouted for encores like a drunk,
emptied my purse in her lap. She cackled,
raking it in, 'I did tell God this morning
to give me something.'

Susanne Ehrhardt

Lambskin

Write me a lambsong,
sing me a skin, yellow curls
coming through, curling to wool,
to warmth, long as a long tongue licking me –
filling my cells with milk.

We stole the lambskin –
I roll on its song,
we took its song, its young song,
unrolled the curves
laid them over our flat hills.

She places me at the core
where its heart grew –
I am naked in a pool of wool
floating my bones in chambers of air,
lamb wool singing me.

Outside the ewes are calling,
I am the cry and she comes.

Sarah Westcott

For the Woman who goes Swimming every Day

No longer of earth, she is liquid now:
the water around her frees her to float.
As long as she's in that air gone element,
she is buoyant as clouds, acrobatic:
a trapeze artist dancing the high wire.

All embracing it holds her, there is no one
to say what shape she should make.
Small children are fishes, their mothers
anemone shoals loosed from rock pools.
Arms and legs are white underwater
like porcelain or a new born's skin.

She can be who she wishes:
queen of the depths, not of the ground.
All gestures are hers, she has a view to
the bottom and top. Who says she is not
a siren of the deep?
All breath and sinew,
words float away to reflections.

With each stroke she pushes back
against all that is dark, swimming lengths,
catching sun, making her own choreography,
an original dance,

become a girl in the first month of summer,
at the first place of knowing,
in the silence, restored.

Clare Crossman

Song

who is the woman
whose washing's in the wind

who stands at the doorway
believing in the wind

as if it were a mystery
which she had seen and named

a mystery slowly filling
each buoyant sheet with sun

the wind is in her sorrow
the wind is in her lungs

who is the woman
who's singing in the wind

the wind that washed her song
lays its breath on her tongue

Jemma Borg

Falling on my Feet

Crow swings on peanuts.
In the cold and bright,
he looks like a black flag.

The sun has come out,
a lemon light that happens
at this time of year.

I am falling on my feet,
coming to land, the hush of the breath,
all things written through with light.

Rose Cook

After Green

One summer not so far from here,
when all the botanists had lost
their leafy voices, when mothers
had dulled and withered

into an endangered species, crackling
through the dust-walled valleys
because their sons had flooded
into the river and escaped like an army

of petals on the raft of its back,
when dreams turned grassy,
when fear had run dry,
there grew a longing, a thirst,

to drift away as only the newborn can,
to be lowered into a basket
and willowed slowly asleep.

Anne Ryland

Simile

Like waking on a clear day early, satisfied with sleep,
and stretching, when the stretch takes you and widens you further
than the narrow arches of the body knew they could go,
widens you and flings you softly to your furthest of touch –

this simile that I know and don't know, that won't attach,
that's like the moth I found on the floor, white, plumy, perfect
except that something had gone out of it; or else perhaps
a flawless immobility had crept in; and this moth

resembles the dream whose loss I wake to, that's telling me
the vital thing I need to know which waking displaces,
like the smell of a loved body that once seemed like the smell
of love itself and now you can't, can't recall. Can't recall.

M R Peacocke

Reward for Winter

For the first time in her adult life,
she allowed herself to sweat, to leave
dust under her fingernails, to be
imprecise. As spring leached into
summer, heat snaked through pores
and found her chilly core that
hadn't seen daylight or action
in years. No amount of SPF could
block her thaw once it started;
the field licked folds of her mind
with a green velvet tongue.
Every night she inhaled the sky,
tasted clouds and stars, heard
ten million blades of grass sing
for rain. She stroked the dark like
a cat, rubbed against rough wooden
fence posts till warmth spread inside
out, urging her on. And when she came
back to herself, she could smell every
animal she'd touched on her fingers,
their oils and dirt mixed with her own.
She'd never felt so loose, so unfinished

Di Slaney

Antarctica to Tamazepam

When people asked what her problem was
she insisted *late nights* –

even though she tip-toed upstairs with her mug
of milk and manuka honey

and sprayed her bed with *Jujube Dreamy Pillow Spray*
and stopped her ears with yellow foam

against next door's miniature schnauzer
and recited all the places in the world

beginning and ending in A
until her head was a maze of A's

and practised the Zen of transmuting thoughts
into logs floating along the Yangtze River –

nothing worked. So now she reaches for the bottle
with the amazing name

and with a pill poised on the tip of her tongue
she unplugs her ears and waits for her thoughts

to dissolve like sugar cubes lobbed into
Yellowstone's Lone Star Geyser.

Maggie Sawkins

Waking Elegy

A hand is sliding the dolls forward slowly
out of sleep. They begin to take their places

on the windowsill. The pawns are moved up
into the sunrise and slowly I remember

there are gaps on the chess table that can't be filled,
moves that can never be made again.

Opening myself to the sounds of the ivy garden
where the rustle of squirrels muffles

the terracotta armies in the earth
and distant birds sing of God's election plan

and the lost embroidered routes,
I try to hold back a while longer, to stay hidden,

not yet move into the world of 'and then'
where a boy at a desk is still

doing his word puzzle, making loops
around the letters word by word.

Sue MacIntyre

Pastoral

Beethoven's pastoral symphony tonight
    alive on my radio

and it's the second movement
    and all the dead people I know

arrive and begin to dance a waltz
    upon some luminous stretch of sand

and all their endearing ways
    and eccentricities merge

revolve in my mind
    enlivened by the plaintive tones

of clarinet and piccolo,
    the swirling bass notes' drone

and as they dance   the tide as it always must
    races towards the shore

combines with my salty tears
    and as the music ends

I know I will have to watch
    as each one of them drowns again

Genista Lewes

Epiphany

The scent of burning hair
drifts through the room.
I see my mother cutting off
the extra inches from
her long grey plaits,
singeing the tips
at the candle on the shelf
and as she quickly pinches
the blazing ends to put them out,
I wonder, what would happen
if they caught alight?
Then as she winds the plaits
over her hidden ears,
stabbing the hairpins in
to keep in place
the silver snail-shell coils,
I see her crowned with fire,
a golden coronet of flames,
transformed.

Pat Watson

She sits straight-backed, hands stilled.
Day drains out of the kitchen,
chrysanthemums on the table glow
with the last of it. She listens.

She knows the silence is a thin skin
over the sounds she wants to hear,
its surface can be puckered, broken.
Once – unless she dreamt it – she heard

footsteps' certain progress down the lane,
the familiar change of pitch as they reached
the yard. Then silence claimed them.
She knows she must not will it.

She must wait. But she cannot stop
her mind seeing the hand reach
for the latch, lift it; the door swing
inwards; then his figure at the threshold.

She cannot stop her mind and his face is
so pale, his mouth a bruised berry,
his eyes smudged stars. How taut
his body is, braced against her longing.

Cynthia Fuller

The mushroom shed

If they come back
my mother will materialize
in her armchair, a book
fluttering its new white wings

but my father will walk through the garden
looking critically at everything:
the unswept leaves, the ground elder
sneaking on to the lawn.

I think the shy scalps
of the carrots will please him,
also the birdtable
with its offering of crumbled rice

but the moment I wait for
is when he eases open the door
and steps into darkness.

He's back on the mountainside
among the mushroom plots
roped off for neighbours.
The old watchman, Koma, lets him through.

The smell of the mushrooms
is everywhere – he kneels
among the braille of pineneedles
hoping to uncover their whole bald world...

as here, by the empty trays,
I watch his fingers silently questioning
and, little again, I crouch
close to him, almost behind him,
to see what he sees.

Dorothy Yamamoto

The Bee-Swarm

I dream we're running, stumbling over
the cattle-pocked ridges
of a dried-up marsh.

The wired air stacks current,
prickles rise on our arms;
dark sky squats close to earth.

We reach the oak woods, sprint past
the great oaks, chestnuts, fast,
not to be trapped under trees in storm –

you stop. And point. I pull you by the arm.
No, you say, *look!*
Alive as a broken ant-hill

a huge melanoma
heaving with cell division,
hugs the shoulders of the oak.

Bees crawl, pour across each other,
wings loud in the crackling air:
a storm of insects, thunder clouds of black.
I put my hand out, wanting to touch.

But my hand is stopped
by a sudden flash as the first
lightning zaps its neon
helter-skelter through the trees,

shocks the wood electric green.
Now it is you who pull me
by the arm: hand in hand

we race through the woods
as the first great drops begin to fall.

All the way I fight the strong
desire to look back.

Gill McEvoy

In The Neuadd Valley, Brecon Beacons

Here in the hall I first heard it, these mountains a bowl
Of green and golden, blustery clouds
Pouring over the moor. And I lay down
Not far from the horses, and called to them.
Slowly they approached, trusting and not trusting the sound,
Hooves wavering. High above us mewed a bird of prey.
The grasses rustled. It seemed the horses drowsed,
Dreamed. Now a great stillness settled.
And, as we dreamt, red dunes rose up,
Set fast to rock, were eked away by rain and rivers;
Glaciers built, and gouged steep gorges
Down the mountain's flank, then faded
In a rising summer mist.

And yet the horses did not move at all.

At last one mare stepped out, thrust her muzzle close
Till I could feel her hot breath on my hair.

So it began.

Not voice, animal cry nor instrument
But something living, making out of time
A sound, as if beyond the thresholds
I could hear the song of all that is,
One single, constant, unadulterated note
And me, and horse, and mountain
Held and threaded on that perfect bow.

What sweetness, sudden and immediate,
Lying in the grass was; just to be
And listen, my mind opening and closing upon eternity.

Hilary Davies

Visitation

In the garden a young woodpecker
is eating birdseed; he stretches from the branch
or hangs upside-down from the feeder
edging the seeds out with his pointed beak.
Later he pecks among the husks on the grass
and visits the walnut-tree like a blessing
bestowed without thought or motive, a free gift.

At night I summon him inside my head;
he opens his chequered wings, angelic,
and his crimson cap distracts me from fear.

Mary MacRae

Life's Work

Less need now to cry out your life in art

as if you are finally large enough to contain
your darkness and your blazing

or to recognise how small you are

and how it doesn't matter

though it seems to matter that you see,
picked out in slant autumn sunlight

three white gulls
perfect as porcelain

coasting on shaky reflections in water

already murky with evening.

Caroline Natzler

Cautious

There are other conversations we might have had,
As we met on the hill: the one about Mr Brown,
Or the new gate. But we talk about the weather,
As usual, and whether his washing will get wet.

There are other ways home I could have taken:
Through the houses, perhaps, or along the main road.
But I take the usual one, through the trees,
Down the hill where the blackberries grow.

Sometimes these bits of life, unspoken, unvisited,
Move shyly forward, as if their time has come.
We take a rougher road or talk of harder things.
The going's not so easy, but the views are good.

Yet further back again, some other time, the
Dark inconceivable, the vast unimagined
Lumbers towards the light, shouldering
Certainties aside, casting new shadows.

R V Bailey

Aberaeron
    for Jean Porteous

Like a great cat, the moon licks up the sea.
Small boats in the harbour clatter and bob,
Like dancers on the night before Waterloo.

The tide goes out, comes in, and lovers
Idle along the edge, old dogs
Lagging behind, young dogs sprinting ahead.

Beyond the bridge, serene squadrons of ducks
Navigate between moorings. A grizzled man
Walks, and stops. Watches the water. And passes on.

The ferryman has retired, but he'll be back.
Like a lighthouse the church stands
On the highest place. *Katy Lou, Seren Las,*

Y Marchog, Bingo perch on mud,
Then take to water, ready for anything.
Bright painted houses. Sea shining out beyond the bar,

Waiting quietly to do something violent.

U A Fanthorpe

Quiet Street

Dwell-time
along the quietest street in London,
no one speaks
of the death of the walnut tree.

Footfall time
along this quiet street,
a woman waits in her kitchen
for her husband to go to the tennis club
so she can read Paradise Lost
aloud to herself.

Put an island on my breakfast plate
the day I turn wise,
plus the deeds to a diamond mine
in the back of wherever,
be kind to me like that.

Down-time
along this quiet London street,
time to remember
his eagle's grip on happiness,
trees in Richmond Park,
the sky's lovely struggle with light,
a day full of too many days.

Penelope Shuttle

Acknowledgements

The poems in this anthology are reprinted from the following books, all by permission of the publishers listed or of the poet where copyright rests solely with the poet. Thanks are due to all the copyright holders cited below, and to all poets included, for their kind permission.

Anna Adams: *Everlasting Expanding Rings 1, Scarp Song* and *The Self Portrait,* from *Open Doors* (ed John Killick) (Shoestring Press, 2014)
Moniza Alvi: *Hanging,* from *Europa* (Bloodaxe Books, 2008)
Margaret Beston: *Silence,* from *Long Reach River* (Indigo Dreams, 2013)
Jemma Borg: *Relic, Song* and *The mathematician,* from *The Illuminated World* (Eyewear Publishing, 2014)
Joanna Boulter: *Dyeing the Corpse's Hair* and *My Father's Life in a Glass Coffin,* from *Blue Horse* (Vane Women Press, 2014)
Elizabeth Burns: *A Life,* from *Clay* (Wayleave Press, 2015); *Sea-campion,* from *The Lantern Bearers* (Shoestring Press, 2007); *White,* from *Held* (Polygon, 2012)
Judith Cair: *Raku,* from *The Ship's Eye* (Pighog Press, 2013)
Anne Caldwell: *Slug Language,* from *Talking With The Dead* (Cinnamon Press, 2011)
Anne Cluysenaar: *January 1* and *February 27,* from *Touching Distances: Diary Poems* (Cinnamon Press, 2014)
Carole Coates: *Crazy Days 9,* from *Crazy Days* (Wayleave Press, 2014)
Rose Cook: *Falling on my Feet* and *One Thousand Birds,* from *Notes From A Bright Field* (Cultured Llama, 2013)
Jill Eulalie Dawson: *Owl,* from *Hearting Spread With A Slow Hand* (The Littoral Press, 2012)
Kerry Darbishire: *Bringing in the Shrimps* and *Rainstorm,* from *A Lift Of Wings* (Indigo Dreams, 2014)
Joan Downar: *An Afternoon,* from *Various Returns: A Selection of Posthumous Poems* (ed Michael Paine) (Shoestring Press, 2014)
Jane Duran: *Leggings, 1936,* from *Silences From The Spanish Civil War* (Enitharmon Press, 2002)
Margaret Eddershaw: *Sandstorm,* from *Catching Light,* (Poetry Space, 2013)
Susanne Ehrhardt: *Song,* from *Rumpelstiltskin's Price* (Templar Poetry, 2011)
U A Fanthorpe: *Aberaeron* and *The Beasts,* from *New And Collected Poems* (Enitharmon Press, 2010)
Janet Fisher: *Arlo's Song, On Reading War Poetry While Listening To Jazz* and *Voyagers,* from *Life And Other Terms* (Shoestring Press, 2014)
Kate Foley: *A Perfect Rain,* from *One Window North* (Shoestring Press, 2012)
Wendy French: *Red Sarong,* from *Splintering The Dark* (Rockingham Press, 2005)
Cynthia Fuller: *By Way of Silence* and *Crossbar,* from *Estuary* (Red Squirrel Press, 2015)

Jacqueline Gabbitas: *Stigmaria,* from *Earthworks* (Stonewood Press, 2012)

Katherine Gallagher: *Jet Lag* and, from *After Kandinsky, 8 Tension in Red – (1926),* from *Carnival Edge: New & Selected Poems* (Arc Publications, 2010)

Daphne Gloag: *The radio clock,* from *Beginnings And Other Poems* (Cinnamon Press, 2013)

Rebecca Goss: *Virginity,* from *The Anatomy Of Structures* (Flambard Press, 2010)

Lucy Hamilton: *Mal Culottée,* from *Sonnets For My Mother* (Hearing Eye, 2009)

Jean Harrison: *Elegy,* from *Terrain* (Cinnamon Press, 2010)

Alison Hill: *Dandelion Time,* from *Slate Rising* (Indigo Dreams, 2014)

Sheila Hillier: *London Light,* from *A Quechua Confession Manual* (Cinnamon Press, 2010); *Visit from the Sourcier,* from *Hotel Moonmilk* (Eyewear Publishing, 2013)

Rebecca Hubbard: *Physic Garden XV* and *Physic Garden XVIII,* from *The Garden Of Shadow And Delight* (Cinnamon Press, 2014)

Rosie Jackson: *Recovery Stroke, Room of the Three Windows* and *The Lovers' Exchange,* from *What The Ground Holds* (Poetry Salzburg, 2014)

Carolyn Jess-Cooke: *My Father's Mother,* from *Boom!* (Seren Books, 2014)

Pauline Keith: *In the dark stable,* from *By The Light Of Day* (Wayleave Press, 2014)

Victoria Kennefick: *Archaeology,* from *White Whale* (Southword Editions, 2015)

Bernie Kenny: *April 10th, 1929,* from *These Are My Days* (Boland Press, 2015)

Mimi Khalvati: *Knifefish, Snow is, The Pear Tree* and *What it Was,* from *Earthshine* (Smith/Doorstop Books, 2013), republished in *The Weather Wheel* (Carcanet Press, 2014)

Angela Kirby: *Foxholes, Scaling the Herrings* and *Syszygy,* from *A Scent Of Winter* (Shoestring Press, 2013)

Jane Kirwan: *Without Resolution,* from *The Man Who Sold Mirrors* (Rockingham Press, 2002)

Wendy Klein: *I Greet the Blue Water Buffalo of Cambodia,* a version of this poem appears in *Anything In Turquoise* (Cinnamon Press, 2013)

Lotte Kramer: *Birthday Poem for My Mother,* from *New And Collected Poems* (Rockingham Press, 2011)

Angela Leighton: *Hollyhocks,* from *The Messages* (Shoestring Press, 2012)

S J Litherland: *The Discovery,* from *The Absolute Bonus Of Rain* (Flambard Press, 2010)

Eleanor Livingstone: *Snow Hare* and *The Soul,* from *Even The Sea* (Red Squirrel Press, 2010)

Melinda Lovell: *Face to Face, Past the Rose Hips* and *West,* from *Walking The Hillside* (Waterloo Press, 2015)

Sue MacIntyre: *Deep Forest, Remembering Elephants, Sunflower Harvest* and *Waking Elegy,* from *The Wind Today* (Hearing Eye, 2010)

Mary MacRae: *Life Story,* from *As Birds Do* (Second Light Publications, 2007); *Visitation,* from *Inside The Brightness Of Red* (Second Light Publications, 2010)

Gill McEvoy: *In the Dry Season, The Bee-Swarm* and *The Plucking Shed,* from *The Plucking Shed* (Cinnamon Press, 2010)

Jennifer A McGowan: *Shambles,* from *The Weight Of Coming Home* (Indigo Dreams, 2015)

Caroline Maldonado: *The Lost Library of Jesi* and *Two redstarts,* from *What They Say In Avenale* (Indigo Dreams, 2014)

Nancy Mattson: *Learning the Letter Щ* and *Pencil Stubs,* from *Finns and Amazons* (Arrowhead Press, 2012)

Hilary Menos: *Wheelbarrow Farm,* from *Red Devon* (Seren Books, 2013)

Rosie Miles: *My Daughter,* from *Cuts* (HappenStance, 2015)

Helen Moore: *apples are not the only gadgets,* from *Ecozoa* (Permanent Publications, 2015)

Kim Moore: *All My Thoughts, And The Soul* and *The Knowing,* from *The Art Of Falling* (Seren Books, 2015)

Jenny Morris: *Twilight,* from *Keeping Secrets* (Cinnamon Press, 2015)

Sharon Morris: *Indwelling,* from *Gospel Oak* (Enitharmon Press, 2013)

Caroline Natzler: *January* and *Life's Work,* from *Fold* (Hearing Eye, 2014)

Gill Nicholson: *All These Heavy Books,* from *The Buoyancy Of Space* (Hen Run, 2014); *Portuguese Visitors In New York,* from *Naming Dusk In Dead Languages* (Handstand Press, 2009)

Maggie Norton: *A Late Love Poem,* from *Onions and Other Intentions* (Indigo Dreams, 2012)

Carolyn O'Connell: *Ripened,* from *Timelines* (Indigo Dreams, 2014)

Helen Overell: *From behind her,* from *Thumbprints* (Oversteps Books, 2015)

Fiona Owen: *Man O' War* and *My Father,* from *The Green Gate* (Cinnamon Press, 2015)

Mandy Pannett: *Garnet for Birth,* from *All The Invisibles* (SPM Publications, 2012)

Rennie Parker: *Butterwick Low,* from *Candleshoe* (Shoestring Press, 2014)

Linda Rose Parkes: *Husband Sewing* and *My Inner Ear,* from *Familiars* (Hearing Eye, 2014); *whenever the van pulls up,* from *Night Horses* (Hearing Eye, 2010)

M R Peacocke: *In Slow Motion,* and *Notes on a Bonfire,* from *Caliban Dancing* (Shoestring Press, 2011); *Simile,* from *In Praise Of Aunts* (Peterloo, 2008)

Jo Peters: *Daisy,* from *Play* (Otley Word Feast Press, 2015)

Pascale Petit: *A Tray of Frozen Songbirds, Black Jaguar at Twilight* and *Blackbird,* from *Fauverie* (Seren Books, 2014)

Ann Phillips: *Rose Petals,* from *Walking the Wall* (Poetry Workshop Publications, 2010)

Deryn Rees-Jones: *A Chinese Lacquer Egg, Meteor* and *Trilobite,* from *Burying The Wren* (Seren Books, 2012)

Laurna Robertson: *Kiss,* from *Praise Song* (HappenStance, 2014)

Sue Rose: *Damage,* from *The Cost of Keys* (Cinnamon Press, 2014)

Jane Routh: *The Eleventh Hour,* from *Teach Yourself Mapmaking* (Smith/Doorstop, 2006)

Elisabeth Rowe: *Blue,* from *Thin Ice* (Oversteps Books, 2010)

Anne Ryland: *After Green* and *Never so much as larva,* from *The Unmothering Class* (Arrowhead Press, 2011)

Julie Sampson: *Somewhere,* from *Tessitura* (Shearsman Books, 2013)

Maggie Sawkins: *Antarctica to Tamazepam* and *Sub Title: A Visual Exploration of Fetish,* from *Zones Of Avoidance* (Cinnamon Press, 2015)

Myra Schneider: *Lost,* from *The Door To Colour* (Enitharmon Press, 2014); *Seeing the Kingfisher,* from *Circling The Core* (Enitharmon Press, 2008)

Ann Segrave: *Mudlark,* from *Persimmon* (Oversteps Books, 2014)

Seni Seneviratne: *L'inconnue De La Seine,* from *The Heart Of It* (Peepal Tree Press, 2012)

Jill Sharp: *Untouchable,* from *Ye gods* (Indigo Dreams, 2015)

Hilda Sheehan: *Nudibranch,* from *The Night My Sister Went To Hollywood* (Cultured Llama, 2013)

Penelope Shuttle: *Quiet Street,* from *In The Snowy Air* (Templar Poetry, 2014); *Task,* from *Redgrove's Wife* (Bloodaxe Books, 2006)

Hylda Sims: *Strangers,* from *Sayling The Babel* (Hearing Eye, 2006)

Susan Jane Sims: *Birds in his Head,* from *A number of things you should know* (Indigo Dreams, 2015)

Anne Stewart: *Nightscape,* from *The Janus Hour* (Oversteps Books, 2010); *Snow snow more cold lonely snow,* from *Only Here Till Friday* (Bibliotecha Universalis, 2015)

Janet Sutherland: *Cicatrice* and *Five things I saw before my mother died,* from *Hangman's Acre* (Shearsman Books, 2009)

Kay Syrad: *Burnt Island Lake* and *Letter from my Brother,* from *Double Edge* (Pighog Press, 2012)

Fiona Ritchie Walker: *Northern Territory,* from *The Second Week Of The Soap* (Red Squirrel Press, 2013)

Jean Watkins: *Boatbuilder, Honeysuckle Sides,* and *Shinglebacks,* from *Scrimshaw* (Two Rivers Press, 2013)

Pat Watson: *Epiphany,* from *Landscape With Figures* (Cedar Press, 2013)

Rosy Wilson: *When you dream stone, I dream water...,* from *Bright Water Over Grey Stones* (Lapwing Publications, 2014)

Lynne Wycherley: *Glacier-Walk, Inhabiting a Distance,* and *Solstice,* from *Listening to Light: New & Selected Poems* (Shoestring Press, 2014)

Pam Zinnemann-Hope: *Translation of a Letter from Grossvater Erich to My Mother,* from *On Cigarette Papers* (Ward Wood Publishing, 2012)

Editors, *Fanfare*

Wendy French was Poet in Residence at the Macmillan Cancer Centre UCLH from April 2014 to May 2015. She has published three collections of poetry, *Splintering the Dark* with Rockingham press, *surely you know this*, Tall Lighthouse press and *Born in the NHS*, Hippocrates press. The latter is a reflection on what it is like to grow up in doctors' households and to work for the NHS. It is a mixture of fact, memoir, anecdote and poetry. This book is the result of a collaboration between herself and Jane Kirwan and is co-authored.

Dilys Wood founded Second Light Network in 1994. Her collections are *Women Come to a Death* (Katabasis, 1997) and *Antarctica* (Greendale Press, 2008). She has co-edited Second Light's ARTEMISpoetry and the following anthologies: *Her Wings of Glass* (Second Light Publications, 2014), *Images of Women* (Arrowhead Press in association with Second Light, 2006), *My Mother Threw Knives* (Second Light Publications, 2006), *Four Caves of the Heart* (Second Light Publications, 2004), *Making Worlds* (Headland with Second Light, 2003) and *Parents* (Enitharmon Press, 2000).

SECOND LIGHT PUBLICATIONS

FANFARE

is a sister publication to anthology:

HER WINGS OF GLASS

eds. Myra Schneider, Penelope Shuttle and Dilys Wood

retail £12.95 OFFERS, incl p&p, quote ref 'Fanfare'
£9 Second Light members * £10 non-Members (UK) *
£12 non-Members (outside UK)

The focus is on women's writing which deals with 'big issues': the future of the planet, good and evil, aspects of our relationship with the natural world and with each other, different aspects of our imaginative understanding of 'who we are'...

Second Light Publications, 2014, ISBN 978-0-9927088-0-1

ENCOUNTERS with the natural world * SAVING THE PLANET * WAR ON HUMANITY
THE HUMAN FAMILY Suffering & Surviving * THE HEART'S AFFECTIONS
MAKING: Creativity and Invention * LOOKING FOR MEANING
IMAGINATION: Visions, Dreams, Imaginings

211 pages featuring 134 women poets, 237 poems

---

and ... *HER WINGS OF GLASS* REMOTE WORKSHOPS

KICK-START YOUR POETRY
WITH WORKSHOPS AT YOUR LEISURE

for poets from beginners to experienced writers looking for new stimulus

work at your own pace at home * work-sharing option
8 workshops of 2-4 hours + * 40+ poets reporting good results
completed poems by women are eligible for submission to ARTEMISpoetry

"highly beneficial, thoughtful workshops, well-paced", Ruth Hill, Canada

Based on Second Light's anthology *Her Wings of Glass,* a course of poetry study –
£40 incl. anthology or £60 for tutors, incl. 5 copies.

contact Anne Stewart +44(0) 1689 811394 editor@poetrypf.co.uk.

OTHER BOOKS FROM
SECOND LIGHT PUBLICATIONS

IMAGES OF WOMEN: "This is a book that has been waiting to be written since, perhaps, the nineteen-seventies, when women at last began to play a serious part in the world of poetry. These images of women are images of women by women, constructed out of twenty-first century consciousness, unmediated by the male gaze." U A Fanthorpe

Arrowhead Press in assoc. with Second Light, 2006, eds. Myra Schneider and Dilys Wood. ISBN 10: 1-904852-14-9 ISBN 13: 978-1-904852-14-8, £12.95, (211 pp)

INSIDE THE BRIGHTNESS OF RED, by MARY MACRAE

"... so strong is her empathy with all living things, so intense her desire to be fully alive ... an extraordinarily coherent body of work" Mimi Khalvati

Second Light Publications, 2010 £5.95 ISBN: 978-0-9546934-8-0

WHAT WOMEN WANT, by MYRA SCHNEIDER
"... Humming with Wordsworth's "force which rolls through all things" (quoted in her poem Cropthorne Church) Schneider has faith in the power of words to affect change." Esther Morgan

Second Light Publications, 2012, £6.95 (48pp). ISBN 978-0-9546934-9-7

BECOMING, by MYRA SCHNEIDER – a book-length narrative poem:
" ... the highly individual voices of four people as they help each other to escape from intricate patterns of prejudice, frustration and self-doubt ... evocative descriptions engage the imagination. ... recaptures ... the neglected ground of dramatic narrative." Anne Cluysenaar

Second Light Publications, 2007. ISBN: 0-9546934-2-6, £5.95, (47pp)

Second Light network for women poets

What do I get if I join Second Light Network?

Opportunities for publication and readings, two copies a year of the 60pp+ women poets' journal, ARTEMISpoetry, plus a full page presence for each member on the Second Light website, **www.secondlightlive.co.uk**, and discounted prices for Second Light books. There are also festivals with workshops and a residential course each year where priority booking is given to members.

"SECOND LIGHT is affirming and creative, thoughtful and wide-ranging. It is unique in offering practical advice, support, activities geared to promoting visibility and publication outlets for older women poets."
Katherine Gallagher

Full membership (women 40 and over), £25pa* Associate membership (women 30 – 40), £16 pa.* Full details of benefits, Membership *discount options and joiners' application form at www.secondlightlive.co.uk
Founder: Dilys Wood Consultant: Myra Schneider Administrator: Anne Stewart

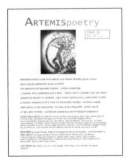

ARTEMISpoetry

twice-yearly women's poetry journal

Second Light Publications
www.secondlightlive.co.uk/artemis.shtml

a biannual journal of women's poetry and women's writing about poetry (Reviews, Interviews, Feature Articles), Second Light & Second Light members' news and women's artwork.

"...certain to become a must-have, must-read journal for all involved with contemporary poetry..."

Penelope Shuttle

Annual Subscription, 2 issues, May & November. £9 +p&p. Single Issue, £5 +p&p.